Advance Praise

T0293281

"'Leading by example' may be a thing of the past. Current leaders lead by motivating, encouraging, and supporting their team. In a world where burnout is becoming more common, it is imperative for leaders to constantly undergo self-reflection and assess their inner well-being and take stock of their emotions and encourage their team to do so as well. Emotional pain, if not tackled, could take a toll on innovation and productivity leading to a trickle-down negative effect. This book by Payal Nanjiani helps leaders undergo that much-needed self-reflection and solve the critical problem of productivity."

—*Senthil Radhakrishnan*
Administrative Chief and Clinical Neurosurgical PA
at Duke

"You don't have to own a fancy title to be a leader who others in your organization are willing to follow. Payal gives practical tips to show that a positive attitude and small incremental changes can give you the ability to stand out and lead with or without authority. A must-read for a natural leader at any level!"

—*Michelle Proctor*
Principal Business Operations Officer

"Payal Nanjiani has often helped JKYog conduct leadership workshops. The way she connects with the audience, captures their interest, ignites their imagination, and drives home the message to leave them transformed, is all very inspiring to see. I love her passion for enriching the lives of people and her dedication to her work. In Payal's latest book, she shares profoundly deep insights and amazing motivation for everyone to develop the mindset of leadership."

—Swami Mukundanda
renowned spiritual Guru

"While there is no perfect formula for success as a leader, author Payal provides us with some intriguing insights on how working with our inner self can set us up on the track to be a successful leader."

—Shankari Rajangam, Ph.D., Neuroscientist,
Preston Robert Tisch Brain Tumor Center at Duke

ACHIEVE UNSTOPPABLE SUCCESS IN ANY ECONOMY

ACHIEVE UNSTOPPABLE SUCCESS IN ANY ECONOMY

The 7 Divine Mantras to Maximize Your Leadership Potential

PAYAL NANJIANI

Routledge
Taylor & Francis Group

A PRODUCTIVITY PRESS BOOK

First edition published 2021
by CRC Press
6000 Broken Sound Parkway NW, Suite 300, Boca Raton, FL 33487-2742

and by CRC Press
2 Park Square, Milton Park, Abingdon, Oxon, OX14 4RN

© 2021 Taylor & Francis Group, LLC

CRC Press is an imprint of Taylor & Francis Group, LLC

Reasonable efforts have been made to publish reliable data and information, but the author and publisher cannot assume responsibility for the validity of all materials or the consequences of their use. The authors and publishers have attempted to trace the copyright holders of all material reproduced in this publication and apologize to copyright holders if permission to publish in this form has not been obtained. If any copyright material has not been acknowledged please write and let us know so we may rectify in any future reprint.

Except as permitted under U.S. Copyright Law, no part of this book may be reprinted, reproduced, transmitted, or utilized in any form by any electronic, mechanical, or other means, now known or hereafter invented, including photocopying, microfilming, and recording, or in any information storage or retrieval system, without written permission from the publishers.

For permission to photocopy or use material electronically from this work, access www.copyright.com or contact the Copyright Clearance Center, Inc. (CCC), 222 Rosewood Drive, Danvers, MA 01923, 978-750-8400. For works that are not available on CCC please contact mpkbookspermissions@tandf.co.uk

Trademark notice: Product or corporate names may be trademarks or registered trademarks, and are used only for identification and explanation without intent to infringe.

ISBN: 978-0-367-49490-2 (hbk)
ISBN: 978-0-367-49434-6 (pbk)
ISBN: 978-1-003-04676-9 (ebk)

Typeset in Garamond
by codeMantra

The way to success is through your inner leader

Most of all, to my husband, Ashish Nanjiani,
Celebrating togetherness, now and always

Contents

Acknowledgments

Thank you to the thousands of leaders and entrepreneurs around the world who learned and at times challenged the leadership mantras, thus sharpening my thinking.

To the participants who have attended my keynotes and workshops, I have learned much from you.

To Dr. Arun Arora, CEO of Edvance and a true mentor and friend under whose guidance I have grown and progressed.

To my parents—my mother Laltoo Malkani and my father Ashok Malkani both who gave me unconditional love.

To my Success Is Within team, for their loyalty and dedication on every project and assignment to ensure that each client gets the best leadership content and service from us.

To WKNC 88.1-Geet Bazaar, our media partners.

To Productivity Press, Taylor & Francis Group for trusting in me and making this book reach its highest potential.

Most importantly, to the higher power, the universe, that guides all hopes and magnifies all good things.

Author

Payal Nanjiani is the world's leading Indian-American motivational leadership and success mastery speaker and advisor. She is the founder of *Success Is Within Leadership*, a coaching and training company with a vision to inspire maximum organizations and people lead and succeed regardless of their title. For nearly twenty years, Payal's work has been embraced by Fortune 500 companies, mid-size organizations, management institutions, celebrity CEOs, entrepreneurs, government officials, and universities. Her aim is to help maximum people in the professional sphere to be successful and lead a fulfilled career life—be it in business or job.

Organizations and CEOs call Payal to develop world-class leaders and create a culture that improves both productivity and profits. She is known for developing world-class leaders who can succeed and grow the organization—no matter what. Through her leadership keynotes, workshops, books, and coaching, she has to date influenced more than a million people and organizations around the globe.

Payal's first book *Success Is Within* has reached people worldwide, making her a true global phenomenon for helping people achieve success with speed and serenity. Alongside this, she has created a high impact on women's leadership growth. Her podcast "iSucceed" has inspired women globally to step up their leadership.

Payal lives with her motto "Success Is Within" and believes that success can be achieved with speed and serenity in any economy. She lives, plays, and works in the North Carolina area of the United States and on stages around the world. She can be reached at success@payalnanjiani.com

www.payalnanjiani.com

Also by Payal Nanjiani:

Success Is Within: The 21 Ways for Achieving Results, Prosperity, and Fulfillment by Changing Your Leadership Mindset

Gathering insights from twenty years of the author's executive coaching in the United States and abroad, this book presents twenty-one mindfulness strategies for business leaders, corporate heads, entrepreneurs, and professionals. During the author's coaching sessions for business and corporate leaders and her trainings at corporations, mid-sized businesses, small businesses, and start-up organizations, she discovered that there is a wide gap between those who achieve success and those who do not. This gap indicates that there is still something significant missing in the business world. *Success Is Within* fills this gap by encouraging business professionals to "mind the mind."

Success Is Within Coaching

As a result of *Success Is Within* coaching, executives, entrepreneurs, women, and individual contributors have been able to successfully navigate the realities of the workplace with speed and serenity. In today's high-pressure work environment, *Success Is Within* coaching has a direct and positive impact on your behavior, actions, and results. It transforms you deeply from within, and you become a master in your game. Payal is known for helping her clients achieve their results within five coaching sessions.

Success Is Within Workshops and Keynotes

Companies are witnessing a massive positive and lasting change in the behavior of their employees and an increase in their financial outcomes as a result of the *Success Is Within* workshops. Innovation and speed of implementation have improved massively. Corporate teams and leaders are now able to intentionally and consciously define, articulate, and influence their self-leadership and interpersonal leadership towards achieving greater outcomes.

Would you want to bring these results to your company? Reach out to Payal and her team at success@payalnanjiani.com.

Success Is Within for Women

Payal has customized corporate programs to support women's leadership efforts in the workplace. She has significantly enhanced the economic achievements of thousands of women globally, encouraging them to climb the corporate ladder, succeed in business, and realize their true potential. Her podcast channel "iSucceed" is dedicated to inspiring women in jobs and business.

Introduction: The I-Power

Why do we have too few exceptional leaders in any organization and in the world at large? Why do so few succeed in business and in their jobs? Why do some people generate fabulous results, while others just scrape by? These are some of the million-dollar leadership questions circulating today inside companies and around the world. These very questions led to my quest for answers and formed the springboard for *Success Is Within Leadership*, along with providing the reason for me to write this book. As I reflect on these questions, I am reminded of all the people who want to be successful and exceptional, but say it's nearly impossible. We are in an age where uncertainty in any industry is at its peak, they say; the global business environment is like a pressure cooker, and Wall Street is unforgivable when companies miss quarterly projections.

I find that the majority of employees and entrepreneurs I talk with are working more than ever to survive in this uncertain market. I also believe we are in an age where abundant information on success and leadership is readily available. Resources are at their highest level of availability, and communication is global, quick, and easy. Self-help products are available in abundance. In America alone, we spend $11 billion on self-help products, which include seminars, training, books, and motivational tapes. These trends suggest that a majority of people in the world should be successful today. But the statistics tell us that only 1% of the world population is successful. In general, only

20% of an organization's workforce does 80% of the crucial work. So, what about the remaining people? Let me tell you, most people are working hard, upgrading their skills, and doing what it takes to get there. Yet the gap exists, persists, and is only increasing. If information, ideas, and positive thinking were all that was needed, then this gap wouldn't exist. Everyone would be happily fulfilling their dreams. Two decades of my work and life have been dedicated to reducing this gap and helping everyone attain unstoppable success in their jobs and businesses regardless of the economy or their role and title.

I've been around some incredible leaders over the past decade, and what I have observed is that apart from being skilled in their craft, they have developed one of the most imperative, but often neglected qualities of success—the ability to be unstoppable. Given today's business environment, we have to be leaders who can achieve one goal after another, regardless of economic or other circumstances.

Yes, we need leaders who

- keep going in the face of setbacks and breakdowns;
- decide that failure or job hopping are not long-term options;
- always focus on the possibilities rather than the challenges.

The Concept of I-Power

A lot of people these days are good at what they do. Some are even elite. A select few are even unstoppable. But unstoppable is more about being than doing. In order to achieve unstoppable success in any economy, you must know firsthand how to *be* an unstoppable leader—to do this, you must focus on your I-Power. Each of the seven billion people on this planet has this power. However, only a few people have explored and awakened it. Are you asking yourself what this power is all about? I-Power represents the power of your inner leader. For some years now I have been revolutionizing the concept of leadership by evangelizing the idea of inner leader to companies and individuals. The results are miraculous. There is an inner leader who guides us and helps us navigate through all our challenges to reach our goal. Whatever you manifest in your work life is a result of how your inner leader operates. When you see someone bounce back soon after a major setback, it's because of their inner leader. And when you come across people who give up easily or lead a stressful life, it's also because of their inner leader. And how do we access this inner leader? Do you need a guru or spiritual master to find it? The truth is that we all have access to this force of our inner leader. The time has come to provide a common approach that enables everyone to display leadership and succeed in whatever they do. In order to achieve unstoppable success, you must begin to work on your own inner leadership powers. Hear me out now: leadership is not just the domain of people with titles and official positions. Leadership is not reserved to the CEO or CFO. Leadership is every*body's* business. The number of "bodies" working in your organization equals the total number of leaders your organization has. If you are a solopreneur, you are a leader first and then an entrepreneur. Whatever work you do, to achieve unstoppable success your first business is to develop your leadership mindset.

Let me tell you how I derived the concept of inner leader, a practice that is helping individuals all across the globe to achieve unstoppable success. It is enabling companies and businesses to develop a culture of "A" players and champions where regardless of a person's role or title in the organization, everybody shows leadership. It is serving entrepreneurs to achieve profitable and organic growth. It is for individuals to personally grow as leaders. Around six years ago, while visiting a friend of mine who works in aerospace research in Seattle, I heard from her how potential astronaut candidates undergo one of the world's most intensive training regimens. In order to survive and work in the demanding environment of space, they undergo a two-year physical and mental preparation program. Through the utilization of interdisciplinary space knowledge, they are well prepared to deal with a much higher degree of problems in anticipation. While concentrating on their target of reaching outer space, their inner focus is on how to keep themselves mentally healthy and happy in this very tough environment. As I left that conversation with my friend, my mind began to delve deeper into what she had said. I came to understand that for the space mission to be a success, the astronaut has to be powerful both in their skillset and mindset. They must be highly adaptable to deal with the uncertainties of surviving while in space. Everything from food to space walks revolves around the well-being of the astronaut, not the mission itself. I also observed this inner focus in high-performance athletes. Everything revolves around themselves first—their attitudes, feelings, motivations—their state of mind. I observed that the belief around their work is that if you are internally strong, everything else falls in place—the numbers, the targets, everything.

As I continued to travel, speak, and train, my observations became more precise, and what surprised me most was that the business world does not follow this same priority of being internally strong, happy, and healthy. We overlook the reality that we too are functioning daily in a dynamic and demanding work environment, even if you are not doing space walks or climbing mountains. You also need to be inwardly strong, but the task-oriented business world revolves around productivity and targets, not around the individual entrepreneur or leader-manager. Growing powerful leaders is the key to growing a powerful business.

Have you observed a construction site? The first step is construction site preparation, which often takes months to accomplish. What about a personal project like gardening? To have a beautiful garden, you have to begin by clearing the area and raking the soil to prepare the ground for the seed to be planted. Even in the face of a major windstorm, there are always some trees and buildings that stand firmly while others are destroyed. Their roots or foundations are deeper and hold the ground firmly. It's all in the roots, the foundation. Building such foundations takes a very long time, though, so patience and resilience are integral ingredients in the path to success.

You too have dreams. You have goals. You want to believe deep down in your soul that you have the power to make a difference, that you can become successful, and that you can live a fulfilled life. Your success also lies in your roots in this case—your inner leader. However, we do not normally spend time preparing this ground for success. For real long-term success, it's imperative to build a leadership mindset, regardless of your title and position. Look around you today. Most people are cranking through a lot of work, and they're doing what they have to do to meet expectations and deadlines. Most people are surviving, not thriving. If you look under the mental hood, you'll see boredom, frustration, stress, broken relationships, lack of confidence, widespread loneliness, and workplace depression. Our current leadership training and corporate benefits aren't helping us cope up with these everyday realities. In an article published in American Psychology Association, Chief Executive Officer Norman B. Anderson, Ph.D., writes that America is at a critical crossroads when it comes to stress. A recent study by Korn Ferry Institute says that stress keeps getting worse, and the more it piles up, the more difficult life becomes for company owners and workers alike. You may blame today's work environment for your failures and stress, but that truly will not help you. With time and technology scurrying along at a rapid pace, challenges and problems in our lives are only going to increase. The solution to the dilemma? Build a stronger inner leader who can deal with every and any situation on the outside (just like the astronauts).

I draw the solution of inner leader further out of my physics class. Physics speaks about resilience as the *power to resume an original shape or position after compression.* Similarly, in a work culture that celebrates the external it's very important for you to develop yourself internally in ways that allow you to return to happiness and success after a difficult situation or event. We live in a world of challenge and competition. No matter who we are or what our circumstances in life, we all encounter tough times. But nature has also provided the remedy for this problem within each of us. Have you heard of self-repair materials? Self-repair materials are synthetic substances with the built-in ability to automatically repair damage to themselves without any external diagnosis of the problem or human intervention.

Similarly, nature has provided you with a built-in self-repair ability—the inner leader. Why then is the subject of inner power so consistently diminished or ignored at the corporate level, where it is most needed? Look around. Who do you see in your workplace? People, you might say. I see power. When you hire people, you're not simply hiring bodies with skill sets. You are hiring mind power. The number of minds working in organizations today is powerful enough to take any organizations to great heights in the market. But because we ignore inner leader power, we operate in a zone of averages, and organizations do not see massive results. We are so disconnected from our inner leader that we aren't able to operate at our peak. When people in the organization aren't operating at their peak, the company culture will feel the impact, and so will the company's clients—affecting their trust in the organization and its capacity to deliver. When you see a few people who stand head and shoulders above their peers, know it's because they have trained their inner leader.

I began to do more research on the effects of applying I-Power with many of my clients, and the results were mind-blowing. People who were stuck in the same roles for many years began to show movement in the company. Organizations were able to see growth and higher profits. Innovation increased. Individuals were inspired to lead and succeed in whatever they did. Millennials, who are the drivers of the digital revolution, got a deeper understanding of the leadership mindset. Building on this power has resulted in a ten-fold increase in productivity, less staff turnover, and more revenue. We neglect I-Power in leadership to the detriment of our business success and personal well-being. The seven mantras I share with you in this book will help you to strengthen your inner leader—the I-Power, build a magnificent leadership mindset, apply the self-repair techniques, and achieve unstoppable success in life.

The Exceptional Leader

An interesting question I often get asked is, "who is an exceptional leader?" Is it someone who has more money and power? Or is it the one who builds a business empire or becomes the CEO of a Fortune 500 company? Well, by criteria of their visible status, they might be considered exceptional leaders. But let me take you beyond status and position and share with you the true essence of an exceptional leader. In the early years of my work life, when my job was to hire people for company operations, I admired great resumes filled with degrees in different disciplines. I looked up to the people who generated wealth. However, over a period of time, I observed these same people who were bright and intellectual often turned out also to be unfocused, unwilling to commit, lacking persistence, and had a hard time dealing with pressure and uncertainty. They would easily lose their confidence, begin to panic, get burnt out, and then spiral downward into a hole of self-doubt. I found myself still looking for truly exceptional leaders. I found that exceptional leaders are the ones who are *highly inner-self-directed people*. They are the ones who have brought about real change in their thinking and behaviors. They can regulate and adapt their behavior and thinking to the demands of a situation to achieve goals that also mesh with their values. By contrast, average leaders feel they are governed by the organizations, people, circumstances, and situations in which they happen to find themselves. Today, we need more transformed and highly inner-self-directed leaders and entrepreneurs. Today's leaders are everywhere, not just in government offices or corporate boardrooms. They are teachers, personal trainers, coaches, parents, artists, spiritual gurus, and just individuals choosing to better themselves.

I wrote this book for one purpose: to create a wake-up call for individuals and companies to change the way they approach the human side of business, of leadership, and of success. Our society and the world at large cannot continue to withstand the deepening shortage of exceptional leaders and the increasing gap between the successful few and the unsuccessful many. Let's address this challenge in new ways to develop more exceptional leaders at all social and economic levels who can deal with the immense complexities of our twenty-first-century world. This book serves as a guide to an organic growth of people who lead and succeed regardless of the economy. This book should help you recession-proof yourself and thrive in any economic environment. More than ever it's time to develop and apply I-Power to turn your dreams into reality and for every individual and organization to become a success.

The greatest obstacle to success is the self. Most of us struggle to lead ourselves and often give up during tough times. As a leader, you are the manager of your work and of your life. You will have to make quick and tough decisions; you will have to live with the success or failure of those decisions. This book is designed to help you become a highly inner-self-directed individual and take your leadership and business to the highest level in every economy that you pass through. It is the solution to increasing the number of exceptional leaders and successful people in the world. It will help you to craft an extraordinary life and dominate in any economy. It is bound to help you unlock the leadership secrets to creating a life of fulfillment, purpose, and meaning. Once you master the seven proven mantras in this book, you will begin to develop a strong I-Power and maximize your time, energy, and resources to better sculpt an extraordinary work life. It is filled with equations and formulas that will help you calculate your success rate. You will discover how to strategically direct your emotions to leverage your potential.

This book offers you seven divine mantras that will enable you and your people to move through hardship and achieve unstoppable success. Let me tell you something interesting about the word *mantra*. A mantra is a sacred Sanskrit word and is considered to possess mystical or spiritual efficacy. *Man* means "mind," and *tra* means "to liberate." Mantras are statements repeated frequently that have the power to free your mind from negativity and invite in positive change. Once you begin to meditate on these or any other mantras, they can create a profound difference in your inner leader, which then impacts your outer results. I know it might be hard for you to believe that merely by repeating and practicing the mantra of surrender in this book, you can immediately achieve more productivity in your work, or by working on the mantra of action that you can powerfully change your level of results. Each chapter ends with a powerful mantra for you to meditate on and apply in your day-to-day work life. It will strengthen your I-Power.

Becoming Unstoppable

The critical elements of modern leadership involve resilience, persistence, high energy, optimism, self-awareness, the desire to go beyond, creativity, risk-taking, mindfulness, and a willingness to learn from a fluid situation to emerge with strategies that suit the overall growth of an organization. One cannot adapt to the new leadership culture in a technologically disruptive environment by continuing to practice old-school leadership patterns. As I reflect on the professional paths of legendary leaders in my two decades of work with them, I see an inextricable connection between their professional behaviors and their inner leader. In turbulent circumstances, where others may have been uncomfortable, they held a thoughtful and reflective posture.

Here is an equation that will help you calculate your own annual rate of unstoppable success:

$$\text{Unstoppable success rate} = \frac{\#\text{ of times you bounced back after failures (I Power)}}{\text{Total }\#\text{ of failures}} \times 100$$

The media call me a motivational leadership guru. I am no guru. I am like you and everyone else who has had their share of successes and failures. I have frustrations, struggles, and fears that I share throughout my books. I am always learning and progressing. I have learned a great deal about human behavior and mindset from my real-life gurus: my father, my mentors, the scriptures, other books, and my own experiences. I do believe that success is your birthright. And that to be a great leader, you've first got to be a great person. A true leader and a successful person is the one who considers work as *dharma* (divine duty) and *dharma* as work. Work is divine. It defines you and influences your life. It's time to enjoy your work. It's time to celebrate the divinity of your work. It's time to celebrate your I-Power—the inner leader within you.

As you begin to master these seven divine leadership mantras and apply them in your own life, you will be amazed at the transformation they will have on you and on the people around you. As Confucius said, "our greatest glory is not in never falling, but in rising every time we fall." You have the power, *your* I-Power to rise higher than ever before.

All my life I have been working, coaching, and speaking with legendary leaders and champions in industry. We see these elite performers make success look effortless. But just as a swan gracefully moves along the water, we do not see its hard paddling beneath. Similarly, you don't see the practices and rituals that take place below the surface of the success of these "A" players in the world. Through this book, I am deconstructing those practices and rituals that take place below the surface of successful people and bringing it to you in simple, doable language. And when you become famous and achieve your heart's desire using these practices, remember that you've made someone proud and that someone is rooting for your success—the universe and me. Make sure to drop me a line. I'd love to hear from you.

PART 1

The Core of Your Leadership and Unstoppable Success

Who Am I?

About 2,600 years ago, when Siddhartha Gautama (later the Buddha) sat down under the Bodhi tree, his resolve was to realize his true nature. Siddhartha had a profound interest in truth, and the questions "Who am I?" and "What is reality?" urged him to look even more deeply within and shine a light on his own awareness. The answers led to his enlightenment. "Who am I?" A simple question, you might say. Well, how would *you* answer it? With your name, your family pedigree, your job, or your income? The business world gives us many titles—manager, engineer, cardiologist, server, doctor, coach, entrepreneur, or speaker. No doubt, these roles are real. But once you begin to identify yourself with your titles, positions, income, car, office space, company name, and business, they become your identity. And that externally based identity manipulates your thinking and behavior. Our titles and roles constantly change with time. The truth is that you are known as a leader *because* you have a team. You are an entrepreneur *because* you have a product or service to offer. You are a doctor *because* you have patients. So everything you believe yourself to be is dependent on something else outside of yourself. As you get attached to these titles and roles, you begin to identify yourself with them.

Dave's Story

Some years ago, during my speaking engagements, I met people from different parts of the world and saw the importance of the "Who am I?" question. At one point, I met a young man, Dave, at one of the conferences I was speaking at in Australia. He must have been in his early thirties. My talk was centered around "Unstoppable Leadership Success" and how leaders can apply the I-Power to build their business and team. During a networking break, Dave came to meet with me. He said if only he had heard about the I-Power earlier, his results would have been different. Earlier in his career, Dave had been climbing the corporate ladder at high speed. Within just a few years of his hiring, he was named as the youngest vice president in the history of the company. People surrounded him for advice; he was called upon at various public conferences to speak about his success. Office colleagues waited at airports and hotel lobbies to personally pick him up; everyone offered him the best service ever. One night while driving home from a late-night meeting, Dave's car met with a brutal accident. The accident caused Dave serious brain damage that led to aphasia. Aphasia is a language impairment that affects the production or comprehension of speech and the ability to read or write. Doctors said he was lucky to survive, but it took him three years to get his speech back enough to be understood, and it still continues to remain distorted to some extent. He continued to work at the same company but had to step down to the level of an individual contributor. Outwardly, Dave appears to work earnestly at his job, but internally, his world remains shattered. He moves from one day to another with no enthusiasm and hates the fact that he no longer receives those accolades and service. People no longer ask for his advice, and he could see no future for himself in the workplace. After hearing my talk, he experienced a leadership breakthrough. He realized he wasn't just that role or title. That he wasn't the income he receives or the accolades he gets. He is much beyond. Dave promised himself to apply my program's mantras in his life.

Alex's Story

That same year I also had an opportunity to meet Alex, the CEO of a well-known company in Singapore. During our lunch meeting, he said something deep that really got my attention. He said that whatever name and fame he has received is not for him. It's for the title that he holds. The day this title is gone, everything that came with it would go too; everything, except the self. You will take yourself with you everywhere. I observed that Alex navigated through all his work pressures by knowing himself internally.

Anil's Story

As 2009 was wrapping up, I had the opportunity to coach Anil, a manager from a Fortune 500 company. He was determined to move ahead and achieve his goals with speed and also serenity. Every day he would drive himself to work, drop his daughter at school, do all his day-to-day duties, and at the same time, aspire to reach to the next level in his career. He would go the extra mile to invest time and money on his personal development. And above all, he was a person who always smiled. You may say, "What is so great about what he does?" Well, only two years before, Anil had been brutally bitten by a shark at the beach. He survived, but both of his arms had to be amputated. His arms may have been removed, but his determination wasn't. He bounced back within just a few months and has been taking over many aspects of his former life. He knew he is beyond this body.

Speaking with Dave, Alex, Anil, and many others like them, I realized that there is power in the question—"Who am I?" Because we do not know our real self, we do not see the reality of who we are and can be. We allow people and situations to define us. We are always chasing shadows. We hold on too tightly to whatever we possess, and the fear of losing it keeps us in fear each day. Instead of believing in our core self-identity, we believe our identity originates outside of ourselves in titles, business, and income. This state is called *maya*. Maya means "illusion." We are so focused on day-to-day operations and doing what we believe needs to be done that we don't see other challenges coming. And when they do come and enter into our lives, they shatter most of us. They break us from within and then all the accolades, titles, and fame that we have become attached to seem to leave us feeling lonely. And then depression, anxiety, stress, burnout, loneliness, and sadness enter into our lives. But some leaders do not break from within when life happens. They move ahead. They believe in themselves and aren't afraid of losing what the business world has bestowed on them. Challenges do not break them; challenges *make* them. These leaders reach the category of the "successful few." They are highly inner-directed. They are unstoppable. This is because they know deep within who they truly are. All the negativity and tension in the corporate world today is because of not knowing who we truly are. When you do not know who you truly are, economic shifts are going to adversely impact your life. From an individual contributor to the CEO of large organizations, this question remains hugely unanswered today. We are just moving on, shifting from one role to another, fulfilling the demands of our jobs, completing our to-do lists, meeting people, and just finishing the day. In the daily grind of work life, we often forget to pause and ask this profound question ourselves: "Who am I?" It will take leaders with a different way of thinking to reinvent leadership in business.

To thrive in the face of relentless change, complexity and uncertainty, you need to address this question, and you should dig deeper into yourself every time you ask it. It is also a question that builds an organization's culture, and it will likely cause you to begin to question your role in the organization. You may start to design your own personal branding. But if you don't know who you truly are, do you know anything else for sure? If you don't know who you are, will you be capable of truly knowing your team and your clients? You are shifting unconsciously from one persona to the next all the time. The only way to unveil reality is to know your true identity. There is nowhere else to search for the answer to this deep question except within yourself. What you think the self is, is what ego is, an imagined story of who you think you are based on social conditioning.

Knowing yourself is a journey. It is not a quick, leisurely activity. It's also not about finding what your favorite color or passion is. Knowing yourself is about discovering who you are as a human being, the *real* you. In the day-to-day work of keeping up with your roles and titles, you've lost your real self. Let's say, for example, you are a coach like me, interacting with thousands of people globally. And let's say, for instance, that one of your qualities is to be cheerful. So you smile at your clients, you greet people more often than most others do, and for those who respond positively to you, you reciprocate more positively. And then some people do not smile back at you and you reciprocate negatively to them. Now, say a potential client wants to hire you as a coach. He checks for references. One group of people tell him that you are a great person to work with. You are always cheerful and fun to be around. While another group says that you barely acknowledge them; you are always gloomy. Your potential client now doubts you. My question to you is "Who are you?" Are you the cheerful person, or are you the gloomy person? Our qualities and behavior often change in response to other people's behavior. With this mirroring behavior, you lose your authentic self. Our fundamental challenge as leaders is to differentiate between Who am I? and What am I? When you answer the first question, you begin to build a more powerful self. And this powerful self becomes an achiever. As the business world becomes more complex and its problems more deeply rooted, answering this question is crucial not only for your success but for your long-term survival. You cannot achieve unstoppable success in any economy without knowing who you truly are. The study of leadership begins with the study of discovering the self. Knowing who you are has a deep connection with your performance.

The Quest for High Performance

Over the past several years, I've received many queries about high performance. Everyone wants to internalize the quality of being a high performer. They are perceived as achievers of unstoppable success. These are people who are game-changers who thrive in any economy. Why do many people fail to consistently sustain high performance? I attribute this problem to a lack of self-worth. Here's a little secret—high performers know and observe themselves closely. They know within who they truly are and this is why these people know their self-worth and it's set to a high level. Consider the actions of this mid-level employee who was invited to sit in on a sales strategy meeting with his company's top executives. Although he was both very smart and efficient, he sat there in fearful silence. It was later revealed that he was intimidated by the presence of executives whom he envisioned as "high in rank" and that perception lowered his own self-worth. Because people don't value themselves highly enough on the inside, they stay in the background and never reach their potential.

The Importance of Self-Worth

In the early stages of my career, when I first came to America, I had a job where I earned $14 an hour for doing stuff that I *thought* I liked. I felt grateful and thought this was the best I could get. But as time wore on, I noticed I was using all kinds of skills that, in their respective marketplaces, fetched much more than $14 an hour. I was suddenly doing employee relations, training, customer value creation strategies, newsletter creation, and marketing. One night while eating dinner with a few friends, I heard them all talk about how well they were paid for the work they did. And when they heard what I was getting, they sowed the seeds of self-worth in my head; they all said, "Are you serious? You should be getting paid three times what you are for what you're doing. They are paying you like a secretary and getting the best of your management skills for far too little." I went home that night and couldn't sleep. Was I worth $14 an hour, or was I worth more? What *was* I worth?

I am happy that I no longer question my worth because I have a clear answer to the "Who am I?" question. But sadly, many people fall into the trap of low self-worth. Such people are readily dismissed as "not good enough" to lead others. And even if they do get some opportunities; their growth is stagnated because they don't believe in themselves. Your performance can never reach its peak if you do not know your self-worth first. Peak performance is a mindset. How you feel about yourself and what you think you are worth affect every aspect of your life.

Have you ever thought about and reflected on these questions: What do you believe you deserve? Do you know your value in your industry, in your organization, among your people? Sure, there are salary calculator tools available, but compensation is only one aspect of your work and value. I am talking here of something deeper. In the Gospel of Matthew, it is rightly said, "So don't be afraid; you are worth more than many sparrows." Most of us don't know our real worth, and this is why we settle for whatever is offered. I remember a story I heard in my middle school years about a young man who went to a sage for help.

Once, a man came to a wise man and complained that he felt worthless and that he didn't want to live anymore. He said that everyone around him said that he was a failure and a fool, and he begged the wise man to help him understand his worth. The teacher took off a ring he was wearing on his little finger and gave it to the boy, saying, "Take the horse out there and ride to the marketplace. Find out for me the worth of this ring but make sure you do not sell it."

The youth took the ring and left. As soon as he got to the marketplace, he stopped by a vegetable seller and checked the ring's worth with him. He looked at the ring with some interest, and said he would offer a pound a carrots for it. The youth thanked him and went ahead. Soon he stopped by a fruit seller and asked him what he would offer for this ring. The fruit seller looked at the ring and said he could offer two bags of apples. The youth went ahead and met a jeweler. The jeweler looked at the ring and said he could give him five thousand dollars for this ring. The youth felt happy, but said to the jeweler that he could not sell the ring. As he went ahead he saw a huge diamond merchant's shop. The youth asked the owner the worth of the ring. The owner took the ring, placed it on a clean silk cloth, looked at it through his magnifying glass and said, "Young man, even if I sell my entire shop I could not buy this ring. It's priceless." Soon the boy mounted his horse and rode back. He entered the room and told the teacher, everything that had happened in the marketplace in regard to this ring. The teacher, after listening to the youth, said, "You are like this ring: a worthy and unique jewel. The only person who can understand your true worth is an expert. Why do you go around expecting that anyone you meet on the street knows your true worth?" So saying, he put the ring back on his little finger.

Most of us behave like this youth. We don't know our worth and we accept whatever worth someone puts on us. If you are going to lead, lead in a way that creates value in the lives of others. In order to add that value, you must know your self-worth first. And this is true for everyone, not just for the trained and educated class of people.

During a seminar in San Francisco, on my taxi ride to the venue, we stopped at a red light and I noticed a beggar standing on the corner with a board that read, "I am homeless and hungry, please help." I rolled down my window and called to her. I asked her how much she wanted that could help her at the moment. The question seemed to shock her. Then, she smiled and said, "A dollar would be great." I took out my wallet and handed her a dollar. The light turned green and my taxi went ahead. I later thought to myself that the beggar could have asked for two dollars or more. I don't know if I would have given her exactly what she might have asked for. But the point here is that in her current situation, she thought one dollar was all that she was worth.

How would you answer the question I presented to the beggar? What value do you place on yourself? Many people are struggling with insecurity, and it's eating away at their ability to make things happen in their lives. How many times have you said to yourself that you can never build a business empire? How many times have you dreamed of doing a triathlon but you didn't because you believed you're terrible at athletics? How many times have you set a goal of getting into that next grade level sooner but were positive you'd never figure it out? Listen, you are only worth as much as you think you are. And you will get only as much as you think you deserve. If you think you're worth $14 an hour, you likely won't strive for more. If you think you're worth more than that, you'll work to confirm that belief. Everything you attract into your life is a reflection of what you feel you are worth and how highly you value yourself in all areas of your life. Let me tell you this; if you feel that other people aren't valuing you, take a look inside and recognize whether or not you're valuing yourself. The way you perceive your value will affect how other people see you. If you truly want to increase your net worth, then begin to first increase your self-worth.

You may have a great vision for your company, great plans for your progress. But if you don't know your self-worth and have not worked on increasing it, you will not progress. As a leader, your job is to remind people of all they are and everything they are meant to be. From now on, make it a priority to remind yourself of all that you are worthy of becoming. When you increase your own self-worth, then you will increase the value of your business and team.

In many of my keynotes and seminars, I talk about the concept of increasing your self-worth. And I usually do it in this simple way that I share with you today through this book. At a recent seminar for sales managers in India, I asked the audience to fill in the blank "I AM _____." Some responses included powerful, ambitious, abundant, courageous, and focused. Others fill it in with ideas like disciplined, healthy, wealthy, leader, and fighter. But some filled it in with negative, stressed, fearful, sad, loser, upset, frustrated, critical, arrogant, anxious, irritated, disconnected, and unhealthy. This exercise clearly shows the variation in people's awareness of who they are. If your self-perception is distorted, then all your attempts to influence others will be misguided. Let me ask you what word you would use to fill in the blank here: "I AM _____." Don't sit back and wait to be discovered. Rather decide for yourself if you are the person who can take your team, organization, and self to the highest level of success. Challenge yourself to build on positive words you would write into that blank. And stay true to your self-worth quality regardless of people's responses and other circumstances. And if the word is negative and a destructive type, pledge that you will work on replacing it with a positive and productive one.

Sara's Story

Sara is an entrepreneur whom I met in Zurich. She had attended my keynote around two years ago in Geneva. There she heard me give one of my most demanded presentations, *Take Charge and Lead*. She also participated in the thirty-minute "I AM _____" self-discovery exercise. She met me after the session, and I remember seeing her as a petite woman with low confidence and sadness. She said that evening she had filled in the blank like this: "I am self-pitying." The moment she wrote this she said there was an "aha" moment. She experienced a true leadership breakthrough. She realized that she was holding onto a useless and destructive emotion. Writing it down made Sara realize that this attitude was the cause of all her problems, personally and professionally. She decided there and then that this wasn't going to be her word and destiny. She took another blue post-it note and wrote on it: "I AM GRATEFUL." When I met her this time in my full-day seminar in Zurich, I noticed that she had changed. She was more confident and showed signs of her success. She said that her transformation from

"I am self-pitying" to "I AM GRATEFUL" had totally changed the game for her. Every day, she would tell herself, "I am grateful." She would repeat this many times a day, especially when she went down the self-pity lane when challenges surrounded her. Every time she said this line to herself, it changed both her body and mind. It built her internal motivation and increased her focus on the good that she had. It led to more creativity in her brain that she used in her business. Today she said she is doing well in her catering business. She often upgrades the "I AM _____" to fill in with new productive words that help her grow.

Take a pause now, and fill in your own word here; I AM _____. This word is your anchor. Whenever you feel lost, whenever your confidence begins to waver and you doubt yourself, immediately recall the word you have written, and it will surely help you to change your state and bounce back into high confidence. If all you do before every situation in your life is to anchor to your desired word, you'll be living the life of your dreams. Knowing who you truly are will strengthen not only individual performance but organizational performance as well. People who do not know who they truly are depend excessively on the approval of others in order to feel good about themselves. This negatively impacts their performance at work. By contrast, people who take the time to answer the fundamental question of "Who am I?" are self-confident and willing to risk the disapproval of others because they trust their own abilities. Being a high performer is definitely an internal thing.

Self-Awareness and the Inner Leader

Ultimately, you and I will have to leave this career platform one day and empty it for the generations to come. At that time, when you look back and ask yourself "Who am I?" what role or title will you give yourself? When we retire or happen to lose our job, our external status is often lost, and many people respond with depression when this happens.

I have worked with people who have lost their titles, roles, possessions, jobs, and even entire businesses. They claim that they don't know who they are. They feel obsolete and useless. So "Who am I?" is *the* most profound question for all leaders, and will sustain them through the ups and downs of their careers.

Ramana Maharshi, an Indian sage, reframed this process of Who am I? as a "self-inquiry" and used it as his principal means to abide in self-awareness. For me, the I-Power represents the *inner leader*. The inner leader is present in each of us. It often lies dormant, though, because we have forgotten about its powers and how to use them to make us successful. To ensure a smooth business and career life, to be unstoppable, one must know how to condition the inner leader. You are at a higher consciousness than you realize. Reflecting and being aware of your inner leader brings you closer to yourself. Everything that shapes your outer environment is a result of your inner leader. The more you are aware of this truth and the more you condition your inner leader, the more you raise your consciousness level and can move ahead in the corporate world with speed and serenity. First look within, at your inner leader, and alter what needs to be altered there. Saint Kabir (an Indian poet) said this very well, "I went to find a bad person, but could not find any. But when I looked within myself, I found no one worse than me." It's like Walt Kelly exclaimed in his Pogo cartoon strip, "We have met the enemy and he is us." In order to be the most valuable person to the team and organization, we have to first vanquish our own inner enemy by knowing who we are. When you dig deep and answer "Who am I?" the quest for high performance ends.

In the words of my mother: "You live only once, so live your life to the fullest. Don't die before death." You get only one life to do miraculous work, to do your best, create a masterpiece, so enjoy every single day at your work and leave your mark.

I Will Go with You

It is my firm belief that you are not in the professional sphere just to survive. You are here to thrive. You are here to fulfill your dreams, goals, and desires. You are here to succeed. Each of us has a finite time in our career life, and we should not leave feeling unfulfilled. When it's time to say goodbye, you must be able to look back at your work life and say to yourself, "I enjoyed every day and every moment." Achieving unstoppable success in your job and career is not rocket science. Success is within *you*. It starts and ends with you.

One of the major reasons success eludes us is that we are constantly searching for it outside, like Ali Hafed did. He lived not far from the River Indus. "He was contented because he was wealthy, and wealthy because he was contented." One day a priest visited Ali Hafed and told him about diamonds:

> Ali Hafed heard all about diamonds, how much they were worth, and went to his bed that night a poor man. He had not lost anything, but he was poor because he was discontented, and discontented because he feared he was poor.
>
> Ali Hafed sold his farm, left his family, and traveled to Palestine and then to Europe searching for diamonds. He did not find them. His health and his wealth failed him. Dejected, he cast himself into the sea.

One day, the man who had purchased Ali Hafed's farm found a curious sparkling stone in a stream that cut through his land. It was a diamond. Digging produced more diamonds—acres of diamonds, in fact.

Are you one of those people who looks for diamonds in faraway places? Is the grass really greener on the other side? Is there an opportunity that has been in front of you all the time, but you aren't seeing it? Perhaps there are diamonds sitting just outside your back door. Your success is not in faraway mountains or over distant seas; it's within *you*. Like Ali Hafed, we often run behind success and search for it outside. Soon, we become a pauper by losing our health, mind, energy, and enthusiasm. Success is within you, within me, and within each of us.

Success does not happen because of the economy, boss, peer, team, client, government, or resources. Yes, these are important elements in supporting success, but they are secondary. The primary reason for success is *you*. Having coached numerous business owners and corporate executives, I have come to realize that there is only one reason why a person succeeds. It is because of the inner leader. It is the single most important element that can take your life on a downward spiral or towards growth and progress. The inner leader is very powerful. It can either make you or break you. It can empower you or disempower you. It can limit your growth or give you limitless growth. It can either stop you or give you unstoppable success.

In the earlier chapters, I explained that I-Power is fundamentally the power of our inner leader. Let's look at the equation below to understand the importance of the inner leader in your success.

$$\text{Results}(R) = \text{Decision}(D) + \text{Action}(A)$$

$$\text{Decision}(D) + \text{Action}(A) = I(\text{Inner leader})$$

$$\text{Therefore, Results}(R) = I(\text{Inner leader})$$

$$R = I$$

Each day you are working towards some results (R). Results are because of the decisions (D) and actions (A) that you take daily. Most people swing between results and actions. They take certain actions, and if the results are not as expected, they work on changing their actions, and the process repeats. This is why even though we put in maximum effort we get mediocre results. We forget that results are because of the inner leader. Whatever is happening inside of your organization or in your life today is a result of what's playing inside of you. How your inner leader guides and mentors you is how you will act and produce. If the inner leader is disturbed, stressed, and full of worry, anxiety, and work pressure, what level of energy will you produce? Low energy. With low energy what types of decisions will you make? Poor decisions, yes. And what actions will you take? Massive or mediocre? Mediocre, of course. And mediocre actions will lead to poor results causing the inner leader to be stressed again.

This is the main reason why despite the best technology, training, and information available today, many businesses fail, and many people remain stuck in their jobs and career for years. The inner leader gives up. But when the inner leader is full of happiness, peace, and fulfillment, you will observe the energy level is at its peak leading to massive actions and fertile results. Everything falls on the *I-inner leader*. As inside so it is in outcomes. You may be an expert in DevOp, Scrum, communication, business strategies, marketing, and sales, and yet fail if the inner leader is not programmed for success. Those who can lead themselves can lead any team and any business in any place on this planet and in any economy. What is interesting to note in the equation is that your final results will also be dependent on some circumstances beyond your control. But if your inner leader is in your control, that's all that matters.

Parker's Story

I learned valuable nuggets of leadership wisdom from a close friend and associate of mine, Parker. During his work with a large automobile company, Parker faced a challenge. Because of his potential and super track record, he was promoted to head of global brands. He now had seven people reporting to him whose number of years of experience was three times his own. Being only thirty-three years of age then, and now their boss, it was a challenge. But Parker not only overcame this challenge, he succeeded in making a winning team with those people. Most of us might have feared this challenge. But not Parker. He attributes his success to one thing—self-change. He says that he worked on his inner self because he knew that he would take himself with him everywhere. He realized that if he could not manage the challenge here, he wouldn't be able to manage it anywhere else either.

Thomas's Story

Thomas (a company CEO) had an experience similar to Parker's. Thomas realized at a very early age that while his peers focused on developing their skills, credentials, and experience, he wanted to concentrate on his personal development. He would invest time and money on developing himself from the inside so he could think better and act faster than most in his company. This gave him a distinct advantage, and it took him only fifteen years to become the CEO of the company. Today, he develops people around him to walk on a similar track of recognizing that you will go with yourself everywhere. Again, it's all about the inner leader.

Most of us forget that whatever the condition of the inner leader, it will go with you. You have troubles? Change your job, your hair, your car, your clothes, or anything else; you are still you. And until you strengthen the leader inside of you, your results will never change. You will keep dragging yourself each day to work and outer circumstances, and people will keep disturbing you, and you will remain weak internally. Any company you join, any project you undertake, and any work you do, there will be challenges aplenty.

In pursuit of climbing the career ladder, attaining more wealth, and power, and in the midst of all competition, we often neglect our inner leader. Remember, though, that your inner leader is the only one that will follow you wherever you go. Care for your skill set and keep it up to date, so you can keep progressing to the fullest. Enjoy your titles and wealth. Cherish your team, your people, and your clients. But don't forget to nourish your inner leader since it is the source of all your life's accomplishments and will prove to be your most faithful friend. Be a role model to yourself and others. It might seem confusing, but to be your own role model is a brilliant idea because it is the basis of everything—relationships, creative expression, growth. It shows that you value the self.

Most of us ignore our inner leader's powers. We do not take the time to strengthen it and nourish it, knowing well enough that in our work life, we all will experience the hard times, competition, success, and happiness. And the power to deal with all these experiences lies within you. The inner leader is your self-repair mechanism. When you are experiencing any problem, when you are feeling broke and broken, when things are against you, and when life seems hard, you can draw strength from the inner leader. The inner leader is extremely powerful, but we reduce its powers with self-criticism, self-doubt, negativity, and worry. You cannot run away from yourself. You have more control over who you are and who you want to become than you have over your surroundings.

The true test of your inner leader comes during times of challenge or happiness. It is when you are very happy or excited that you over-promise and regret it later. It is during challenging times that many people get into addictions or give up on their dreams, with more regrets later. Take this example of resilience: how can an airline survive a government order to ground its entire fleet and shut down for days? After the terrorist attacks in New York on September 11, 2001, all U.S. airlines were faced with this same crisis. One that succeeded through the difficulty was Southwest Airlines, which was already known for its outstanding customer service and positive corporate culture. Southwest's passengers, flight attendants, pilots, and ground crews were stranded all across the country after the attacks. But unlike their competition,

Southwest's leadership did more than just sit and wait. They encouraged employees to leverage their trademark fun approach to business and help stranded customers enjoy themselves at the movies or the local bowling alley. And when the ramifications of the shutdown forced other airlines to cut staff, Southwest's then-CEO, James Parker, announced just three days after September 11, that the company would be keeping all of its employees, as well as issuing a profit-sharing payment. This is because of the CEO's state of mind at the time of crisis. I encourage you to take Parker's example and sit with yourself at the end of every week to do a self-performance review. Ask yourself: What is the state of my inner leader during times of crisis in job or business? How did my inner leader do this week? Where did it fall short? Then, construct your own follow-up steps and outline a development plan for your inner leader. Make sure you briefly note down everything that happens in the week, unless you have an impeccable memory for details. The traits of successful leaders have been established for years, and our work environment has changed and is developing faster than ever. One of the leadership traits that needs to top the list is the ability to condition your inner leader. Every other essential leadership quality follows.

The Leadership Cycle of Success

I grew up in India and received most of my education there. At school I was taught, like most of us, various courses such as math, science, history, and languages. There was also a wide range of electives to choose from—music, art, entrepreneurship, communication. At home, I was encouraged to always work hard on my grades. I was guided to get into a good college, and then, I was encouraged to enter into the corporate race. It is here that I met many like me who had been churned out of the same machine—mental clones who grew up with the same belief: "Stay in school, work hard, get good grades, and go to college. Do these things, work hard, and someday you'll be successful." Now, while you are in the safe cocoon of your parents' home and enjoying the college years, life seems to treat you in an awesome manner. You feel like you're on top of the world, as if you can conquer anything and everything. The true view of life starts when you enter the workforce. For me, math and science weren't much help in corporate life.

All these school lessons were great to build my basic knowledge and skill set. But my foundation remained weak, weak from within. And it remained weak for many whom I met in the workforce. During my education years, no one ever taught me how to condition the self for success, how to never give up, on the importance of being proactive, on the joy of taking risk, on how to set and achieve goals, on the value of building relationships, and on the art of failing and yet bouncing back. Now, I am not against any education system nor against any Mrs. Johnson, sixth-grade teacher. The point is that leadership is an art, and unless you have first learned how to lead yourself, you cannot lead any business or team. This self-leadership development wasn't a part of our curriculum. The only time we heard the word "leadership" was either in the business school or in the workplace. And when we did hear it, the focus was just on outer leadership skills. For most of us, this has been the cycle of life, and we have been proud to pass this legacy to our children and our teams as well. I still observe this method of education in most parts of the world today. We continue to churn out conventional and so-called "thought" leaders who are empty from inside, yet moving ahead from one role to another, from one client to another, still believing that this is how one achieves success. And we expect great innovation and massive results from them. So on one end the world is moving into an era of high-tech and artificial intelligence, and on the other end, we continue to develop conventional-thinking leaders who are afraid that artificial intelligence will take their jobs. Do you see the gap here? The truth is that leadership is an inner game. And ironically, most of us haven't been taught how to play and win that inner game.

Thankfully for me, my father was instrumental in helping me develop my inner leader, and the universe conspired to help me come out of this traditional leadership cycle and get into a progressive one. Throughout my work life, my father made it a point to share his nuggets of wisdom with me so I could break through the traditional leadership cycle. And at every stage, the universe intervened by helping me meet and connect with people who were in the progressive cycle. I feel blessed to now be able to impact millions of leaders, teams, and business owners to step into the progressive leadership cycle and experience results like never before.

Skills and Talents Leadership Cycle

In the traditional cycle of leadership, skill sets and talents are extremely important. There is a belief here that with your skill sets, you can take the necessary actions to get your results. This is great if you want to remain an average company or an average individual. The problem with the traditional leadership cycle is that it limits your ability to produce the results you desire most (Figure 0.1a and b).

Emily's Story

Let me share with you another example from one of my clients. I had completed a two-day workshop at an IT company, and we were moving into our one-on-one coaching sessions with the participants. Emily shared her story with me. Emily worked as a software engineer for a booming company in San Francisco. She was talented and outgoing,

Figure 0.1a   *I will go with you.*

Figure 0.1b   *I will go with you.*

building broad connections not only at her workplace but also outside of it. However, she was constantly frustrated with her boss and was hoping she would get an opportunity to work under another boss. When I asked the reason, she said that at one time she had enthusiastically worked on a high visibility project, going a hundred miles with her team, spending sleepless nights coordinating with overseas teams, and completing the project well before the deadline. She had hoped that her boss would appreciate her efforts and put her up on the visibility map and that she would be in line for a promotion. However, none of this happened. Instead, her boss thanked her and gave her another project to work on. Having her skills and efforts go unacknowledged made Emily feel undervalued. She decided going forward that she would not put in so much effort for a project. She also decided that because she was a female, her boss who was a male, had not been able to connect with her thinking. All this led her to put in less effort for subsequent projects, which slowed her growth in the company. But Emily did not see that her own mental response was creating these consequences. What she saw was her growth being stuck because of her boss and because she was a woman.

Emily and many others like her operate daily in the traditional leadership cycle. You may have the best skill set and highest potential, but your actions and decisions depend purely on the state of your inner leader at that time. A traditional leadership cycle forces you to believe that your success and failure are dependent on outer environment and resources. And then, we hop from one job to another looking for that positive work environment, a supportive boss, and a great team. And when you fail, rather than bouncing back with vigor, our inner leader gives up. And when the inner leader gives up, of what use are your skill sets? Here is how a person in the traditional cycle operates:

#1: Work on your skills, knowledge, and experience.
#2: Take actions and formulate strategies based on skill sets and knowledge.
#3: Focus on the results and outcomes.
#4: Develop the inner leader based on the results.

This is the cycle most of us have grown up with and operate in. Most organizations follow this cycle too. How many times have you told yourself this: "I am lucky to have a boss who appreciates my work?" Or "This time I have a great team and I am sure I will meet the targets." Or "If only I was in Australia my business would have been much better." Now there is nothing wrong in praising or giving credit to your boss or team. However, this is beyond just giving credit. Because we operate in this traditional cycle, we start to *depend* on everyone around us. We feel our success or failure is *because* of the economy, boss, team, and/or country. The traditional leadership cycle emphasizes doing and puts all the weight on action and results. It believes that skill sets and talents are of utmost importance. It develops the inner leader based on your results and outcomes. Which means, if your results are poor and not as per what you expected, you begin to feel low and talk yourself out of success. Basically, you begin to operate with the mindset of a victim, blaming yourself and the situation. And how far can a person with a victim's mindset reach? Now here is the deep understanding that brings you back to the starting point in this cycle: You are the same person—with the best of skills, knowledge, and experience. But because your inner leader is feeing low, it will impact your actions negatively, and the cycle continues. Nothing changes on the results front.

Progressive Leadership Cycle

In the progressive cycle of leadership, skill sets and talents are still important. But there is a belief here that everything starts with *being*. Success and failure start and end with *you*. It is based on the foundation that once you have conditioned the *I*-inner leader for a project or business deal, everything else follows. Your energy level, your focus, your decision-making power, your actions, and your results flow from your mindset and not purely from your skill set. Let's bring Emily into the picture again. If Emily had created a different chain of thoughts, instead of the ones she did, her actions and results would have been different. They would be conducive to her progress. If she had been aware of her inner leader and know how to condition it, her performance in subsequent projects would have surpassed her own expectations. Unlike the traditional cycle, a progressive leadership cycle *starts* with your inner leader. Here is how a person in the progressive cycle operates:

#1: Develop the inner leader and be conscious of the state of the inner leader.

#2: Work on your skills, knowledge, and experience.

#3: Take actions and formulate strategies based on skill sets and knowledge.

#4: Focus on the results and outcomes.

The progressive leadership cycle is where most of us need to make a shift to. Here, you begin to constantly develop your inner leader and be conscious daily of its state. When you do this, you raise your energy level that allows you to follow our passion and work on your skills. You have a new vigor towards taking massive actions and achieve your results. Now, whatever be the result, it does not adversely affect you. You still have renewed energy to take massive actions because you daily work on developing your inner leader and be conscious of its state. The cycle of success continues for you.

My experience speaking and teaching about these cycles at many companies across the globe has proven to me that incorporating the progressive leadership cycle into your work life proves that your results are because of you. It shows that everything falls on the I-Power. Your results are because of the work you do inside ($R=I$). Conditioning the *inner leader* is the first step in your journey to leadership and success. Most organizations spotlight numbers. We must understand that numbers are because of your people. The state in which the majority of your people operate decides your organization's market share. Begin to help yourself and your people to shift towards the progressive leadership cycle.

I Over Why

Many people say that it is important to know your "why" in life—your purpose. But let me ask you this; to discover your purpose, what type of mindset must you be in? When Paula was facing a financial crisis in the fifth year of her business, she was in tension. She had to pay the bills, pay her team, and cover other business and personal costs. She was so anxious to change her current situation that every time you asked her what the purpose of her business was, or why she wanted to close a certain business deal, her answer would be "I want to get out of this mess somehow." She showed up at every conference and workshop in the area, trying to be seen and heard, but never connected with people. Her results did not change for the better. This lack of results was because her motives were not clear, and she was on an expensive chase to increase her self-importance from the outside. This is the same Paula who had previously said and lived up to her why of inspiring, motivating, and encouraging people to live their life to the fullest. What caused her why to change?

We know that purpose is important because it guides our decisions and influences our behavior. Your *why* must come from a sound *I*, though, not an anxious one just trying to get out of a situation. Many times I meet with executives and entrepreneurs who know their why, but when I sit with them and dig deeper into it, they are amazed at how their why is controlled by their emotions and feelings about a situation, product, or service. Every emotion and feeling compels you to a different purpose. Most of the millions of people at work have a goal and know their why with full conviction. Yet statistics show a wide gap between successful people and those who are struggling. There are countless examples of failures, business closures, burnout, and lack of productivity. Was their why not good enough? You cannot articulate a strong and confident why if the *I-inner leader* is weak and disturbed. For the same person, their why is different during good times when their inner leader is calm and relaxed, compared to when they are in a tough and challenging situation when the inner leader is anxious. The *why* is all about the doing, and the *I* is all about the being. The why is dependent on the state of the *I*. Any person who starts with *I* will be able to derive a sound why and take their organization and self to greater heights. Starting with the *I* means you are taking the time to be aware of the condition of your inner leader. The art is in mastering the inner leader and conditioning it to achieve your highest level of success.

Mastering the inner leader is like driving a car. You have control only over the steering wheel; the rest of the car is actually not in your control. Yet, you are able to direct the car to go where you want it to go, because the steering wheel is in your control. The same is true if you just take charge of your steering wheel—your inner leader—and steer it properly, everything else goes with it—your business, your job, your dreams, your goals.

I do not know what your dreams or goals are, but I do know that each of you reading this book has the potential to fulfill your dreams. We all have a tremendous force, a power within us to achieve; the problem is we do not use our power. We come to work each day with a feeling of being powerless. And when you do not use something, what happens? Yes, these powers get rusted. Most of us ignore the power of the inner leader, like the cobbler in this story:

A cobbler lived in a large village and was the only cobbler in town, so he was responsible for repairing the boots of everybody else. However, he didn't have time to repair his own boots. This wasn't a problem at first, but over time, his boots began to fall apart.

While he worked feverishly on the boots of everyone else, his feet got blisters, and he started to limp. His customers started to worry about him, but he reassured them that everything was OK.

However, after a few years, the cobbler's feet were so injured that he could no longer work and no one's boots got repaired. As a consequence, soon the entire town started to limp in pain, all because the cobbler never took the time to repair his own boots.

I shared this story to illustrate a simple principle that is so often disregarded. If you don't look after your inner leader, after a while you'll be no good to anyone else either. Your best purpose, intentions, skills, experience, and knowledge will mean nothing, and you'll be unable to do what you're meant to do. I'm not talking about taking care from outside. Many of us get into self-indulgence activities like spa, vacations, the beach, shopping, dinners. While all of these are great to lighten your pockets and give you temporary relief, they do not help much in the long run. When you are put back into your work environment, you will notice how within just a few weeks, the stress and pressure build up and drain you again. And then, you again get into the self-indulgence. It's a vicious cycle here. Rather, begin taking care and strengthening the inner leader, so that you can overcome any challenges that come your way in your professional life.

In this book, I humbly share with you the seven divine mantras to strengthen the inner leader. It is my assurance that when practiced and applied regularly in the right manner, at the right place and time, you will see the results almost immediately. So, get ready to experience unstoppable success in your career. As you read the next chapters, remember that the I-Power is your inner leader, and these mantras will help you to optimize that inner leader. The only way to increase the number of exceptional leaders in your organization, and the only way to become successful is to build an inner leader that guides, mentors, and coaches you towards becoming unstoppable.

The Journey

In our journey towards success and happiness, and our goals and dreams, we often forget ourselves and get lost in numbers and targets. We get tangled in the web of negativity that pulls us out of reality. Career life is a long journey. It is full of ups and downs. How to succeed and feel fulfilled at the end of it all requires more than credentials, strategies, and skill sets. It requires your inner leader strength. On this journey, as you begin to grow in your job, as your business expands, and as challenges and opportunities increase, you've got to improve, and you've got to move away from day-to-day operations to focus on global strategies and expansion. You've got to motivate your teams and help them succeed, too. No leader and no entrepreneur can do well for its people and stakeholders without first doing well for themselves. We need to be focused on what we want if we really want it. But how can you stay focused when you cannot control what you think? How can you stay focused when you don't have authority over your own inner leader?

Today we are mired in a work environment that is taking a tremendous toll on business and government workers as well as consumers. Strategies and business models that once worked don't anymore. Everywhere people are running scared trying to accumulate the maximum skills and credentials to protect their work. I remember here the words of wisdom from my father: "There is uncertainty in certainty and certainty in uncertainty." Just when you feel that you've figured out everything and that work and the economy seem to be stable is when sudden, unexpected changes take place. And when during these sudden changes, you are absolutely sure that there isn't any hope, and you suddenly see things start to improve. No one can predict precisely what the future holds, but we all have to deal with whatever is ahead. We must be prepared within first. Most people who *seem* to have it all are broken inside. I recall here the CEO who was sitting in his office late one evening, looking tired and drained. His huge office on the thirty-second floor in Manhattan was lonely that day. He was frustrated and angry at himself. As I entered this quiet place for our meeting and walked through the open door of his office, he looked up to me with an anguished on his face and said, "I think they will fire me." I walked up to his desk, and as I was sitting down, he continued, "I worked tirelessly, but we did not meet the targets. I did not meet the stakeholders' expectations. I'm afraid the world tomorrow will see me as a failed CEO." As he completed his sentence, I sat on the chair looking at him and his lavish office. Outwardly, he looked as if he had it all under control. This was our first meeting, and he had wanted to hire me as his coach. He then quickly opened one of his desk drawers, took out two bottles of his prescribed medication, popped them in with water, and took a deep breath. The next day news about his suicide was all over the newspapers and television. The above is a true story of one of my would-be clients. I hear a lot of similar stories of anguish when I speak with CEOs and executives. Social media and *the Wall Street Journal* are unforgiving during these times. There is fierce competition. Whether it is people who are at the top of their game or those who are mid-level or just starting off their careers, an identity crisis and ruminations on self-worth create a constant struggle. The I-Power has never been more needed than it is today. Leaders have got to change themselves before changing others.

It is your journey, your journey to success and leadership. Do you want to reach your destination in stress, frustration, and feeling overwhelmed? Or do you want to reach your dreams and goals with a feeling of fulfillment, happiness, and peace? How you want to complete this journey is up to you and your inner leader.

You need not stay frozen at the level of average. It breaks my heart to see so many people in jobs and businesses who are limiting their own success believing that they cannot be extraordinary. It's sad to see so many people retiring with unfulfilled dreams and goals. I know you had tough times in your business and career life. I get that. You might be feeling things haven't turned out the way you wanted them to. You didn't plan for sudden layoffs, job changes, or business deal failures. You didn't want workplace conflicts and stress. Yet things happened, and they happened when you least expected them. But that should not stop you from fulfilling your dreams. Most of us have become serial killers in the workplace. We continuously and harshly kill our dreams, our goals, our plans, and our future. And while we are at twenty and supposedly thriving, we look like sixty and ready for retirement. And yet there are many whom I have met who are currently in a career they love. They are fully on their game and thriving with energy.

No matter where you are, no matter what the economy is like, and no matter what your circumstances are, remember you are powerful. Powerful beyond your understanding, powerful beyond your fears, and powerful beyond every circumstance. You have unbelievable powers. Each of us has a unique role to play in our career life. You've got to make a great impact, you've got to create history, you've got achieve what you want, and you've got to leave behind a legacy. There is a difference between working, surviving, and thriving.

In the next few chapters of this book, you will come across real experiences, stories, and lessons that we can all use each day. You will read interviews with people I have personally noted who have made it in their industry. This book is about you, and some of the best and unimaginable results in your business and job that you desire. Think about it. Aren't results what you are truly interested in? Maybe you want to change how you think and feel about yourself. Maybe you'd like to be a better leader, entrepreneur, team member, or just a better human being. Maybe you want to increase your income or expand your business. Maybe you want to start a business or climb the corporate ladder. Maybe you want to be a great influencer and speaker. You can get what you want and much more by applying the seven mantras that I share in this book. With these seven mantras, you can change anything you want to change. You can build better workplace relationships, you can be more productive, you can achieve more, you can create more space for innovation and creativity, you can build the career life of your dreams, you can be a successful entrepreneur, you can fulfill those dreams with speed and serenity, and you can increase the quality of your daily work life. You will start to love and enjoy your work days. You will be able to create a positive impact, you will leave behind a legacy, and you will be an achiever in every aspect of your work.

Whatever your situation, wherever you are stuck, however successful you are, and whatever the economic conditions, keep this book handy with you at all times. Changes are happening too soon around us. This book will help you now and, in the years, to come to be self-dependent, to realize that success is within you. Whenever you feel that you need a solution to a problem, whenever you feel low and you need to be raised up, read any mantra from this book and it will take you towards a solution.

One of the things I love most about what I do is the opportunity to unravel the mystery of success and leadership. I'm fascinated with the process of probing below the surface to strengthen the inner leader within each person. We are all on a journey to achieve and fulfill our goals. The journey is yours alone. And while you will meet many people on this journey, know that they are with you for a reason and for a season. Ultimately, you will have to complete this journey on your own. Make sure you finish strong. And to finish strong, you will need to uplift your spirits. You will need to give power to yourself, that power which you already possess in abundance. Yes, I want to tempt you to lead. I want to challenge you to succeed in your job, in your business, and in your life. I want you to grow not only outwardly, not just in titles, money and position, but to grow inwardly. I want you to thrive. Because we live in an uncertain world. And with uncertainty outside, if there is uncertainty inside too, you will get stuck in a rut. The power is within you. Begin to discover your inner leader, and you will begin to truly "walk by faith not by sight." "Ultimately success and failure are nothing but a game of the inside." The more empowered your inner leader is, the better your results will be.

PART 2

Your Personal Unstoppable Success Mantras

MANTRA 1

Take Charge

Success does not discriminate between a man and a woman. For if it did, the *Wall Street Journal* would not carry news of numerous male CEOs failing. I wouldn't be coaching male business entrepreneurs and executives. But success does discriminate based on your level of commitment. It sees if you are merely interested or truly committed. The bottom line is that be it man or woman, everyone wants to achieve success, and those who achieve it must sustain it. What amazes and saddens me is the wide gap between the group of people who have made it to the top and people who are working hard and yet struggling financially and professionally. What is shocking is that people who have been placed in prominent roles aren't able to sustain their success. I have been blessed to have been associated with and served both the successful and the struggling groups of people. And I have also observed how so much has changed in the past several years as companies and individuals struggle to compete in today's fast-paced, hyper-competitive global economy. Large corporations I have worked with are under intense and constant pressure to deliver strong financial results year after year to their shareholders. Everyone is putting in maximum effort but getting minimum results. And what about those who have reached to the top and are very successful in achieving their desired outcome, you may ask?

Robert's Story

Being a high-end executive coach, I have met many CEOs of well-known businesses who have it all yet aren't there internally. Let me share with you an incident about Robert, CEO of a popular soda brand in Europe. His life was full of money, power, and a jet-setting lifestyle. Because of the global nature of his business, running a company had become increasingly complex, with decisions needing to be made around the clock. A global business means global travel, not just exhausting business trips across multiple time zones, but having to relocate for work. While shadowing him during a few coaching sessions, I witnessed that for 80% of the day, his major emotions revolved around frustration, disappointment, anger, irritation, anxiety, and worry. All this led to stress in his body, which was seen in the form of diabetes and a stomach ulcer. Yet, if you were to meet with him, you would probably envy his title, position, and lifestyle. What is striking, as many CEOs have told me, is that they usually fail when it comes to inner strength. The successful people I work with are often burned out and stressed. The end game is that they've got very low energy. In my earlier book, *Success Is Within*, I shared some examples of real leaders from different industries who had faced a severe heart attack or other serious health issues in their early thirties. Who is to blame for this condition of ours? Is it our work environment? Is it the societal pressures to achieve more? Or is it the vision of the American dream that we grew up with? No. No one is responsible for your condition except yourself. Most of us have taken *control*, not taken *charge*. When you take charge, you assume responsibility for success and failure. By contrast, when you take control over a situation, you take a position and expect everyone to follow. Once you take charge of the most critical element of success and leadership, which is your inner leader, you can transform any day and situation into a great one. Let me remind you of what I said in the first few pages of this book; how you feel determines the quality of your decisions and actions. And these determine your end result.

True success in any sphere of your professional life comes when you can achieve your goals with speed and serenity. Both are needed in equal proportion for a holistic success. Looking at today's corporate world, most of us are moving ahead with speed and losing our serenity. Then, in search of peace of mind, we wander from church to temple and hope to find it during the Hawaii vacation. Does a break or an exotic vacation truly rejuvenate us? Does that luxury spa treatment or shopping help us get back to our work with vigor? Honestly, these are helping you only from the outside. The problem is within. This is why in a week or two you are again in the mode of tension and anxiety waiting for the next vacation. We have been conditioned to take care of ourselves from the outside because we believe outside factors are dragging us down. We feel it's the economy, the boss, the teams, the meeting, the work pressure, the deadlines, the projects, the business, the clients, and finally the weather that's causing all the problems. A leader who is disturbed from within will generate average results despite all knowledge and experience. You can't then achieve unstoppable success for yourself or for your organization. You feel powerless and hope for things to be better.

Wishing versus Becoming

A middle-aged man was walking the streets on a wet, windy evening near his suburban home. He was going through something of a mid-life crisis and was feeling a bit dejected about his lack of accomplishments. Every now and then over the past few years, he had heard the news about people he went to school with. Some had gone on to have fascinating careers, some were world-renowned authorities in their field, some had made a fortune, some had amazing family relationships, and they all seemed to be doing better than him, leaving him feeling down and alone.

"I wish I could be great," he muttered to himself as he trudged along.

"Then be great!" said a quiet Voice.

"No, I wish I could be great," the man repeated.

"Then be great!" responded the Voice with increased authority.

"You don't understand," said the man. "I want to be a great dad like Phil."

"Then do what great dads do and be great!" said the Voice.

"You just don't get it, I want to be a great businessman like Harry."

"Then go and do what great business leaders do and be great!" said the Voice.

"What are you talking about? I just want to make a great difference like Jim does."

"Then do what great people do and make a difference in the world."

The man slowed down and then stopped walking.

He looked up and sheepishly asked, "Who are you anyway?"

"I'm the One who made you for greatness, not ordinariness."

"So, what do I do now?" the man inquired.

"Go, do, be. Stop wishing for greatness and just be great. The past is unimportant, it's what you do from now on that matters," replied the Voice.

The man pondered these words as he walked home. As his key went into the lock of his front door, he made a decision. Then, he went inside, into the arms of his family, and nothing was ever the same again.

I share this story with you because I believe that you, me, and everyone on this planet have the capacity to be great. We are made for success. We don't achieve that greatness, not because of lack of resources and definitely not because of lack of people's support. We do not achieve greatness purely because we fail to take charge. This is the single most crucial and often neglected element of leadership and success. In my work with legendary leaders and masters, I have observed these people practice this one mantra very diligently. They take charge. Take charge is not about occupying the seats in the boardroom. Nor is it about controlling everything around you. To take charge means you are not dependent on anyone or any situation for your success. It means you have mastered the art of being highly effective, super productive, and able to deliver the best results regardless of work pressure, economy, your role, or business challenges.

The business world teaches us to take charge of our teams, budget, meetings, projects, company affairs, and accounts. But all of these are secondary. First and foremost, you've got to learn to take charge of your psychology, physiology, biochemistry, thoughts, fears, actions, energy, feelings, emotions, focus, and results. You've got to take charge of the uncertainty that is woven into the fabric of business and success. Today, one receives volumes of information—good and bad—from multiple sources. You can't let all of this affect your emotions. You've got to take charge. Take charge of your *inner leader*. Let me ask you something interesting here that I usually ask my audiences: Do you watch television? Imagine you are watching your favorite show on television and enjoying it when suddenly someone takes the remote control from your hand? What do you feel like doing? Some in my audiences say they feel irritated and feel like snatching the remote back. Ironically, how easily we have given the remote control of our emotions to everyone around us to decide if we will be a success or a failure and if we should feel like a master or a victim, happy or sad. Our inner leader dances to their tune. And we do not attempt to take that remote control back. We allow people to press the button of our emotions and react accordingly. And when this happens, when you allow other people to take charge of your emotions, you deplete your energy. And with depleted energy, you cannot take massive actions and cannot make sound decisions. This begins to show in your results. You have to take charge of your emotions and energy level at your workplace. "A" players and legendary leaders I have worked with never operate in this cycle. They take charge of their inner leader. They hold on to their remote. They would never allow anyone to determine how they should feel or how their day should look. Because they know what adverse consequences do to their results. Think about it—when your inner leader is disturbed for any reason, what is your energy level? Naturally, it's low. Your energy should have been high and applied towards creativity, innovation, and achieving your goal. Now it is depleted in thinking and overthinking about that situation or person and in planning on how you can get even with that coworker. With low energy, the quality of your decisions and actions is inadequate, leading to mediocre results. Leaders are known for their decisions, actions, and results, and if your results are in the red, your success is at stake. And now, work becomes stressful. What I say to my clients that they consider of immeasurable value: *Work on its own is never stressful. It is our inability to manage our inner leader that leads to stress.*

Many people have given away their power to their boss, teams, spouse, family, environment, external influences, and clients. My father once told me a story that went deep within me, and I decided then on to take charge. The story is about Tom. Tom was feeling frustrated when he caught up with his mentor Dwyer for their regular chat.

The Chess Game

"I just feel as though I have no control over my life at the moment. My parents are telling me one thing, my friends are telling me another. Everything keeps changing and I'm not sure what I should be doing next."

Dwyer nodded his head and left the room for a moment, returning with a chess board.

He set it down on the table between them and motioned for Tom to start.

They casually exchanged a few turns without any real intent, before Dwyer spoke for the first time.

"In the game of chess, who are you?"

"At the moment, I feel like a pawn. I'm limited in my movement and don't have much ability," responded Tom.

"Who would you rather be?" Dwyer asked.

"I would rather be the Queen, of course. She can move in any direction and is the most feared piece on the board."

"Are you sure about that?"

"Of course! Isn't it obvious?"

Dwyer sat back from the table for a moment and said in a quiet, yet firm voice,

"You don't want to be the pawn, or the Queen. To be the person you were meant to be, you need to be the player moving the pieces around. Stop being pushed around by others and take charge. There are too many people in this world whose lives are dominated by the decisions of others. Their boss, their parents, their peers, the media, government decisions. You're better than that, step up and take charge! We weren't born to be pieces shuffled around on a board, we were born to positively influence and impact the world around us."

Tom nodded his head and smiled, "Checkmate." With that, he rose from his chair and walked out of Dwyer's cabin six inches taller, determined to change the world.

The RCA Technique

Whose life are you really living? You know deep down that you can become more and achieve more if you keep the remote with you. Never let anyone take charge of your success by giving them control of your emotions. The goals and dreams are yours alone. And live them in whatever way you choose. For how long are you planning to blame everyone for your failures and give credit to everyone for your successes? When will you take the remote back? The important question here is this: Do you know your remote control is with someone else? Here is a simple technique I share with my executive clients who have seen real, measurable results applying the RCA. It is the acronym "RCA," which means reality check analysis. Here is how RCA works. As you wake up each morning, consciously do a RCA on your emotions and feelings. Are you feeling happy, full of joy and passion, or are you starting off feeling lethargic and tense? As you go about the day, see if your feelings and emotions changed due to an event or people's behaviors. If it does, it means your emotions are dependent on outer events and people. They control you and your day. This is why you will find the blame game being played very well in the business world. We blame people, circumstances, budget, or weather for all our moods, failures, and problems. And we hinder our own progress. We fail to become unstoppable. And then navigating through the corporate world becomes stressful. Work on its own is never stressful. Stress is because of our own inability to handle our emotions. We are forever ready to retaliate. What we fail to realize is that in the process, we are depleting our own energy. When you apply RCA technique in your everyday life, you begin to become self-aware of your inner leader.

Taking charge of your inner leader is an imperative skill and mindset that most leaders need today to be successful. Teams often look to leaders for examples of how to behave, especially during times of turmoil and change. Leadership occurs in moments of challenge—not during moments of ease. If leaders want others to be exceptional, then leaders must first *do* something exceptional. This, then, requires leaders to take charge of themselves so that they capture the attention of those they lead and influence them to step up to their responsibilities. When leaders are taking charge of themselves, they are seen as more likable, ethical, and as working in the interest of the organization. To be in charge of one's self means maintaining dignity and composure during times of stress, when things are uncertain, or when faced with conflict or disagreement. It means consciously choosing which emotions are appropriate in any given situation, and avoiding expressing extreme or negative emotions at any time. It's about assuming personal responsibility—doesn't matter if you are an individual contributor or in the C-suite.

To take charge of your inner leader and keep the remote with you, ask yourself these three powerful questions:

1. Do I consider how my response will influence my people?
2. Does showing emotion in this situation help me obtain a productive outcome?
3. What message will this send to the people around me?

Taking Responsibility for the Bricks

During my seminars and coaching sessions, many people share with me their concerns about corporate politics. I think this one element tests the level to which we take charge. Corporate politics means people are always ready to put you down, stab you in the back, talk negatively about you, play favorites, or blame you for things you haven't done. Many who are the victims of corporate politics hate to play this game, but they find it hard not to get angry and frustrated. This is where taking charge plays a critical role. In coaching leaders to navigate through corporate politics, I often share with them this story, which has created a massive impact on their actions when it comes to dealing with corporate political games.

The Buddha was walking into the city market one day, and near the city entrance a bitter old man was sitting on a box glaring at the Buddha, who carried a bright smile on his face. At the sight of him this old man started cursing the Buddha up and down, telling him how pretentious he was, how much better he thought he was and how he did nothing worthy of the air he breathed in this world. But the Buddha simply smiled and kept on walking to the market to get what he needed.

The next day, the Buddha returned to the market and once again the old man was there. This time his cursing intensified;

he screamed and yelled at the Buddha as he walked by, cursing his mother, cursing his father and everyone else in his life. This went on for the rest of the week, and finally as the Buddha was leaving the market, the man came up to him, as his curiosity had simply gotten the best of him.

"Buddha, every day you come here smiling and every day I curse your name, I curse your family and everything you believe in," the old man said, "but every day you enter this city with a smile knowing that I await you with my harsh tongue, and every day you leave through the same entrance with that same smile. I know by speaking to you now that you are not deaf, so why do you keep on smiling while I do nothing but scream the worst things I can think of to your face?"

The Buddha, with the same smile still on his face, looked at the old man and asked, "If I were to bring you a gift tomorrow morning all wrapped up in a beautiful box, would you accept it?"

To which the old man replied, "Absolutely not, I would take nothing from the likes of you!"

"Ah ha," the Buddha replied. "Well if I were to offer you this gift and you were to refuse, then who would this gift belong to?"

"It would still belong to you of course," answered the old man.

And so the same goes with your anger, when I choose not to accept your gift of anger, does it not then remain your own?

This insight can be applied to our world of corporate politics with great effect. Every day you have so many people around you, bringing you gifts that are sometimes hidden in ugly packages. Or some are nicely packed, but inside, there are rotten apples. If you take only one thing out of this story, let it be that you always have a choice. You are in charge here. You can accept or not accept these gifts. It is as simple as that. I see it like this: when someone is rude to you, bad mouths you, or in some way tries to put you down, it is nothing but a brick thrown at you. You can't prevent the bricks from being thrown, of course. What matters most is what do you do with those bricks when they are thrown at you. Your response will show if you are a person who takes charge or gives the remote to others. You can either carry that brick on your head and get yourself all worked up, angry, and upset, and then spend time and effort planning on how to throw that brick back at the one who threw it at you. OR, you can stay calm and keep that brick with you, using it as a stepping stone to make progress. Would you rather expend your energy on putting the other person down or invest that energy in upgrading yourself?

Take charge of your choice like the following two legendary men. The story is told of when Abraham Lincoln became the president of the United States, many pretentious people were very much offended that a shoemaker's son should become the president. On Lincoln's first day in office, as he was about to give his inaugural address, a man stood up. He was a very wealthy landowner. He said, "Mr. Lincoln, you should not forget that your father used to make cabinets for my family." The whole crowd within earshot laughed; they thought that they had made a fool of Lincoln. But Lincoln looked at the man and said, "I know that my father used to make shoes for your family. And there will be many others here because he made shoes the way nobody else can. He was a creator. He poured his whole soul into them. I want to ask you, have you any complaint? Because I know how to make shoes myself; if you have any complaint I can fix them for you. But as far as I know, nobody has ever complained about my father's work. He was a genius, a creator, and I am proud of my father!" The whole crowd was struck dumb. They could not understand what kind of man Abraham Lincoln was.

When Narendra Modi was elected the Prime Minister of India, many people condemned him for being the son of a tea maker and for selling tea himself. However, Modi went ahead with his plans and has had a meteoric rise in Indian politics, catapulting from a chief minister in 2001 to becoming the prime minister in just twelve years. What about you? Do circumstances and people's behaviors easily disturb you? Do you gravitate towards anger when bricks are thrown at you?

When bricks are thrown at you or life seems to be getting disruptive, begin to take charge. Don't waste your time and energy in throwing the brick back or sulking. As big as the task of taking charge of your life can seem, three basic practices lie at the foundation for doing so:

- **Be proactive** by making a move. It's emotions that trap us in a rut, in unhealthy habits. Breaking habits requires, first and foremost, taking action. Make a change. Take a step back and think of what your next best response should be. Always think two steps ahead—like what that person's response to your actions might be, and what your action would be in response to his. Be like an arrow that must be pulled backwards to go ahead with force and speed towards its target. Give yourself that time to prepare your next best move that is useful to you and your company.
- **Be aware** of what happens around you, build great relationships with people and with management teams, and keep your focus on your outcomes.
- **Develop a sense of humor** to deal with the bricks thrown at you. Work life is full of ups and downs, tension, and resolution. The key is to be able to look at life, embrace it, and laugh it out.

And let me share a big leadership secret with you—when people throw stones at you, it's a clear indication that you are growing, that you are on the right path, and that you are the best talent in the room. For someone to climb higher, they need you to move out of the way. And when you start to expend your energy dealing with all the bricks thrown at you, that is when you've given them way because now you are distracted and your precious time is being wasted in planning to throw the brick back taking your focus away from your goal. Navigating through corporate and business politics is a game, and when played well, you do not have to compromise your integrity. You can play honestly and come out clean. So the next time a brick is thrown at you, remember that it's given to you to lay a firm foundation for your growth with it. I encourage you to take a pause here and sincerely ask yourself, "To whom have I given the remote control of my life?" Start to ask yourself this question daily so that you can unplug yourself from the system of mediocrity. Here is a quick formula to help you know if you are in charge of your inner leader:

Take Charge:

$$\frac{\#\ of\ times\ you\ remain\ stable\ today}{Total\ number\ of\ incidents\ (positive\ and\ negative)\ today} \times 100$$

Our lives are determined not by what happens to us, but by how we respond to what happens. Your ability to remain stable regardless of the positive or negative events will determine if you are a person who takes charge. Many of us shy away from taking charge of our life because it's scary to know that whatever happens to us is our responsibility. Most people don't like to take this responsibility. The exceptions are transformed leaders who take charge of their actions and the consequences that follow.

The Power of the Response to Circumstances

The story goes that a young man got picked up by the city cops for some petty crime. As they interrogated him, they figured he was a college dropout, had struggled to find a job, and generally had led a wasted life. He spoke reasonably well and didn't come across as a typical hardened criminal. When they asked him why he had let his life go astray, here's what he had to say. "I grew up in a home where we never had enough money. My father was a drunkard, and he was always beating me and my brother up. We didn't have money to even buy textbooks. And no place in the house to study."

And then he continued, "So what else do you expect would become of my life? It's all because of my father. It's all because of the circumstances in which I grew up!"

Not too far from where that man was picked up by the police, a small function was being arranged to felicitate a young man from the nearby slum who had just topped the entrance exam and secured admission into a prestigious business school.

They asked the boy how he did it, and this is what he had to say: "I grew up in a home where we never had enough money. My father was a drunkard, and he was always beating me and my brother up. We didn't have money to even buy textbooks. And no place in the house to study."

And then he continued, "It was clear to me that if I were going to break out of this rut, I had to work harder, take charge of my life and make my own destiny. And that's what I did!"

As you might have guessed, the two men were brothers, and yet their lives took very different turns. One man chose to blame other people and circumstances for what happened to him. The other man chose to take charge of his own life. Which begs the question: What game are you playing? The blame game or the responsibility one?

The MASS Technique

The job of running a team or a company has gotten tougher over the years. Making business decisions has never been more difficult than it is right now. With technology and the unstable economic climate, you need to make accurate decisions quickly. Don't let your emotions and ego take you to an altitude of 50,000 feet. Bring yourself down to fifty feet, and then consider the situation and make a decision. Begin to take ownership of your inner leader, and then take action to drive the change you are seeking. There's an old saying, "When life gives you a lemon, learn to make lemonade!" Getting the lemon is not under your control. But making the lemonade is completely in your hands. And each one of us can make the lemonade. Here's how. I encourage you to experiment with what I call MASS—*Morning Awakening Signature Schedule*. I, along with my clients, have found a massive change in the way we approach work, situations, people, and the day in general after practicing MASS. This simple practice helps to improve productivity tremendously. Most of us enter into a hectic ritual within seconds of waking up and we never stop. We get onto our phone, check messages and emails, get onto our laptops, or watch the news. Then, we rush through the morning to get to work. All of this sends our brain into a morning panic, with a message that the day ahead is super stressful. So anxiety takes over. Instead, give yourself ten minutes each morning to practice MASS. MASS can be your own personal ritual to help your mind feel good within ten minutes. We often forget that we cannot take charge of the externals unless we first take charge of our self—our mind. To *do* good, you've got to *feel* good. Practicing MASS molds your inner leader to think and guide you to become a legendary, world-class leader and individual.

What should you do in the morning awakening ritual? First, begin to wake up the same time each day. Preferably, early morning like five or six am. Many people wake up depending on how their day is scheduled. So if they have a meeting at ten am, you will see they wake up a little late and then watch TV until it's time for that meeting. This lowers productivity. Set an early time to wake up regardless of the work. Your mind is sharpest during the early morning hours, and it is like fresh clay, ready to be molded the way you want it to. Then, as soon as you wake up, don't run to your gadgets or emails. Right there on your bed say to yourself, "Thank you for this day, I am going to make it a great day." The idea here is to purposefully think power thoughts. Because usually the natural thoughts that come as we awaken are, "I don't want to go to work today. I have too many problems." Counter those thoughts by consciously saying, "It's going to be a great day." Once you are up and done with your morning bathroom routine, find a quiet and relaxed place to sit. You should be alone in that space. Use the first two minute to take deep breaths. Then for the next eight minutes, move on to engage yourself in a PPT—positive personal talk. Science proves that what you say to yourself has everything to do with how you experience people or events, how you perform, and of course how you feel. The idea here is to consciously manage the inner leader, quiet any negative chatter, and direct it to a space of confidence and optimism. When you are in the PPT phase, hypnotize yourself by selecting phrases and words that empower your inner leader. For instance, you may be dealing with a problem, or thinking about a creative idea, or working on a relationship. Let your thoughts on these matters flow something like this: "I am doing the best I can," "I can totally make it through this challenge," and "I can and will give it my all to make it work." Once you start off with these thoughts, it will automatically build and you will see a flow of thoughts that will empower your inner leader and strengthen it. It will give you solutions. Use the last two minutes of the MASS ritual to deep breathe and end with a mantra from this book or any other source. The mantra you choose must be repeated several times in a day so that your brain receives this information and makes it a dominant thought. If you decide to give MASS more than ten minutes, I suggest listening or reading something that takes you to a higher level of accomplishment. This way in ten minutes you are ultra-inspired and ready to take charge of your day. You'll kick-start your creativity, your innovation productivity will soar, and your moods will elevate as your endorphins get released. You are bound to achieve a breakthrough. And above all, it will awaken and enlighten your soul. I've learned that if you take charge of your mornings with the right thoughts, you empower yourself to take charge of the entire day. Circumstances and people aren't able to disturb you.

For companies and individuals to evolve in our fast-paced digital era, they've got to have the ability to see the changes ahead of others and make difficult decisions. I know of many people who have stayed in the same company for years and have difficulty making sound decisions. Decision gridlock can happen to anyone, but it does happen most frequently to leaders who've spent an entire career with one company. The processes have worked, and they're part of the company's day-to-day life—so it takes real courage to make any changes—both professionally and personally. Taking charge of the inner leader by practicing the MASS ritual helps greatly to deal with uncertainty, which is the fundamental leadership challenge of our time.

A Fortune 500 vice president spoke to me one day about having to demote one of his team players. This man was placed in the role of a manager after his credentials, expertise, and knowledge were considered. However, with time, it was observed that he wasn't able to deal effectively with the team and had a hard time navigating fast and complex business changes. After three years of his performance review being average, the company gave him a choice to either take a layoff package or get into an individual contributor role. He chose the latter. On meeting with this person, I found that he wasn't happy with his situation. He worked very hard on enhancing his skills, for example. What was lacking was a strong inner core. He was constantly dependent on other people for solutions. He did not invest the time in thinking and reflecting on his situation. He was busy being caught up in the complexity of every day. His attention was on how to bring up his performance through skill sets. I spoke to him about the concept of taking charge and applying the MASS ritual for the upcoming fifteen days. When I met him after fifteen days, I saw a much more confident person. This one leadership practice of "take charge and lead" using the MASS ritual got him once again into a manager position, but this time with speed and serenity, in the same company.

The world is getting more complex, more uncertain, and is changing at high speed. Seasoned people in organizations today have not been trained to deal with these kinds of changes. The ability to deal with uncertainty is a crucial deciding factor when placing people in certain roles. It's imperative for entrepreneurs and leaders to do a self-check on whether they possess this ability or need to develop it more. This characteristic to detect and adapt to the uncertainty, complexity, and the high speed of change comes only when you develop the habit of taking charge of the inner leader so it guides you in the most effective manner.

Starting today, stop complaining about what's happening in your life. Just stop. And start taking responsibility. Take charge of your life. Become aware that you *can* take charge of your success, you *can* make your dreams a reality, you *can* make a difference in the world, and you *can* live a life of greatness. No one is going to come and save you;

you have to save yourself from a life of mediocrity. Tell yourself that the course of your life will be influenced not by what happens to you, but by what you do about it. Be great. It's like driving a car. You have control only over the steering wheel; the rest of the car is actually not under your direct control. Yet, you are able to direct the car to go where you want it to go because the steering wheel *is* under your control. The same is true of your inner self. If you just take charge of your steering wheel—your inner leader—and steer it properly, everything else will follow it—your business, your job, your dreams and goals.

Our culture and society teach us to be remote controlled. We have learned to put our hands out for everything—blaming people for everything that happens to us and asking for everyone's opinions about our life. Stop putting your hand out. Everyone wants things for free. You've got to put in the work. You've got to grind. You've got to go through the struggle, and you've got to go after it. Take charge. Take charge of the opportunities and challenges. Take charge of the recessions and progressions. Take charge of the successes and failures. Achieving massive productivity, serious success, and spectacular impact isn't that hard. On the contrary, it's easy and doable for anyone. Just get started from the inside.

Here is a mantra to repeat to yourself daily. This mantra will enable you to experience a work life that can be joyous, magnificent, fulfilling, abundant, prosperous, and adventurous.

Mantra: "I take charge of my inner leader today."

MANTRA 2

Act Like a Success

What does it take to overcome decades of confusion, pain, and hardship to step into clarity, passion, and accomplishment? There hasn't been a day in the last five years that I haven't gasped a little or felt a tingle in my belly every time I walk into the lobby of a large organization. As I step inside the front door, I pause, giving myself a slight pinch to make myself realize that my current life of travel and progress is my truth. My life today includes book signings, visiting corporations to deliver keynotes and leadership workshops, meeting government officials, working closely with world-renowned spiritual gurus, speaking in eleven different countries, and helping thousands of people achieve their success. It's definitely gratifying.

More dominant in my memory is a day in 2007 when I found myself sitting in the closet of my room, crying bitterly with my face buried in a towel. I could feel the towel soaked with my tears. I kept asking myself and the universe, "Why does this happen with me, every time? What was I asking for? Only to become successful in my work life. To be of value to people and share my expertise!" In my heart, I knew the universe had gifted me—I was smart, talented, and better at leadership than most. Then, why was it that I never got a stable job? Why was I always on the losing end? All my friends and other people I knew were working and progressing. But my story was different. By the time I settled into a job, either I would outgrow the job too quickly or my husband would opt for a relocation, which made it hard for me to achieve what I truly desired. Everyone who knew me had begun to pity me. Some even condemned or mocked my situation. My family seemed to feel that my stars weren't aligned for success despite my hard work and talent. But I still believed the opposite. I believed, and still do, that each of us is born to be successful. I know that if the universe has given me the talent and skills, if it has still kept me in the game and if it has bestowed upon me passion and commitment towards my work, there has to be a greater purpose to it than a nine-to-five job.

That evening in the closet, I promised myself that it was enough. Enough of crying, enough of self-pity, enough of being condemned, and enough of playing a victim. I decided to give it one more, just one more final try to change my destiny. This time I decided to delve deeper within myself to unveil the bigger purpose. I decided to analyze my past and present situations. And sure enough I got an answer that my purpose wasn't that nine-to-five job. I weighed my strengths and calling, and realized that in all of those years, I had done not just a good job but as people often labeled it, a "magical" job in helping others transform their lives and become game-changing leaders. I took a clear view of my life in the rear-view mirror this time and saw the opportunities the universe had given me compared to my peers and friends. One of them is that from a young age, in my early twenties, I had gotten continuous opportunities to work closely with CEOs and other game-changing leaders. I learned from them those qualities and skills that we do not easily find even in the public domain today. It was time for me to now help many more people become exceptional leaders and achieve success. I took on that role. In those times of struggle, success and prosperity seemed far away. But I had discovered a perspective that truly carried me through. I had the "success" within and soon became well known for sharing "insider techniques."

The Universe Wants to Deliver

One evening when I was at my grandfather's mountain home with my family, I became conscious of how the universe wants to deliver our fondest and deepest desires to us. As we were walking in the mountains, my daughter, then a five year old, suddenly fell and hurt herself; she let out a loud scream, "AAAhhhhhh!!!" To her surprise, she heard her voice repeating, somewhere else in the mountains: "AAAhhhhhh!!!" Curious, she yelled, "It hurts?" She received the answer, "It hurts?" Angered at the response, she screamed, "Idiot!" She received the answer, "Idiot!" As she looked up at me confused as to what was going on, I told her to pay attention to what I said. And then I screamed to the mountain, "I love you!" The voice answered, "I love you!" Again I screamed, "You are great!" The voice answered, "You are great!" I looked at my daughter, and while cleaning her wound, I said to her "This is an *echo*, whatever you say comes back to you."

As I said these words to her, I became aware of how our life works the same way. The universe gives you back everything you say or do. Our life is simply a reflection of our actions. If you want more success, create more success within you. If you want more competence in your team, improve your competence. If you feel people keep cheating each other and no one cares, you will always get into more circumstances where you will be cheated and people will care less for your emotions. This relationship applies to all aspects of life; life will give you back everything you have given to it. The universe is here to support us.

Then, why is it that most of us aren't getting what we want from the universe? It's because our desires keep shifting, and the universe misses the delivery address. In my coaching of organizations and individuals, I have observed how many times in a span of just three months their goals and dreams change. Because of this instability, the universe doesn't know your true desire. Let me share with you a story about Catherine, a client of mine who runs a mentoring program for women in business. When Catherine approached me to coach her to become an exceptional leader so she could expand her business, I asked her to tell me in one sentence what her goal was. She instantly said, "Payal, my goal is to educate more women on entrepreneurship." During the next session, I asked her to articulate her goal precisely, this time in writing. She wrote, "My goal is to earn more money while empowering women." During our leadership call, I asked her again about her goal, and she said, "I want to start online business classes for women this year." Finally, it came down to, "I want to grow my business and earn more money." Do you see the lack of clarity in her desires? And this isn't just the case with Catherine. I can give you ample of real-life incidents of people who set goals, but those goals are unclear and unstable. Today when I deconstruct my career life, I realize I had been following the same pattern for many years—changing my goals (and changing my address) from one job to another (and one country to another). I wasn't stable, steady, and clear. This is what confuses the universe and ultimately keeps your desires unfulfilled. Every time you change your goal, you're re-starting the entire process of becoming successful. Most of us are eager to change our circumstances. For this, we work on our "why's" and "how's." We dedicate our time, money, and effort to pursue our goal. When some time has passed and obstacles begin to set in, we quickly change our goal. You see we are all masters in setting goals and victims in achieving them. And when you change your goal, you change everything around it, and the universe, which is at your command to deliver, changes its path too. The universe doesn't respond well to ambivalence. Wishy-washy dreams create wishy-washy realities.

Many of us go to work each day with a feeling of boredom, frustration, and stress. It's time to change the way you approach your work. It's time to lift your head up and get the universe to deliver success to you. What is needed is crystal clear clarity and steadiness, like a pregnant deer. In a forest, a pregnant deer is about to give birth. She finds a remote field near a strong-flowing river. This seems to be a safe place. Suddenly labor pains begin. At the same moment, dark clouds gather above and lightning starts a forest fire. She looks to her left and sees a hunter with his bow extended pointing at her. To her right, she spots a hungry mountain lion approaching her. What can the pregnant deer do?

> She is in labor!
> What will happen?
> Will the deer survive?
> Will she give birth to a fawn?
> Will the fawn survive?
> Or will everything be burned up by the forest fire?

Will she perish due to the hunter's arrow?

Will she die a horrible death at the jaws of the hungry mountain lion?

She is constrained by the fire on one side and the flowing river on the other and boxed in by her natural predators.

What does she do?

She focuses on giving birth to a new life.

The sequence of events that follows can include:

1. Lightning strikes and blinds the hunter.
2. He releases the arrow, which zips past the deer and strikes the mountain lion.
3. It starts to rain heavily, and the forest fire is slowly doused by the rain.
4. The deer gives birth to a healthy fawn.

In our life too, there are moments of choice when we are confronted on all sides with negative thoughts and possibilities. Some thoughts are so powerful that they overwhelm us. Maybe we can learn from the deer. The priority of the deer, in that given moment, was simply to give birth to a baby. The rest was not in her hands, and any action or reaction that changed her focus would have likely resulted in death or disaster anyway. When you are absolutely clear about what you want, you do not deviate from your plan regardless of the circumstances. Most people go to work without a clear focus on their goal. They aren't clear about their goal nor the organization's goals. Ask yourself. Where is my focus? Am I clear with my goals and desires? Because when you are clear in your mind, and when you are steady, you send a strong message to the universe to deliver to you your dreams.

Leading Change

So how does the universe deliver to you? Is it like a pizza delivery place where you call in your order and it's delivered? Well, no, it's not quite that simple. It's a process that each of us must learn so we can become exceptional and transformed leaders of the future. At the outset, you must remember that the universe delivers to you according to your thoughts and actions. What is important to realize here is that most of the time our thoughts and actions are contrary to what we want. We behave and talk in ways that are the complete opposite of what we want.

I get invited to universities to talk to students and inspire them to be successful leaders. During my conversation with them, I often get to hear that they want to get straight A's but end up with an AB or B score. Well, I don't blame them. Their actions and thoughts are completely different from what they want. They keep saying that studies are so hard and that getting a straight A is nearly impossible. Now, if they are saying and thinking in this way, how do you think their state of mind is? You know it's definitely not conducive to pushing them to put in more effort. On the contrary, they will get the urge to avoid studying and get busy chatting or enjoying with friends. Their mind tells them: "It's no use. It's tough to study and it's not easy to get an A in this subject." How many of us have experienced this in our lives too? We want something, but we behave, think, speak, and act in a completely opposite way.

Recently, on a flight to San Francisco, during the wait at the airport, I was in conversation with a lady who worked as a human resource manager in a law firm. She was sharing with me how frustrated she was with her boss, who held on to all the substantive tasks and passed on only administrative work to her. This lady wanted to get more independent in her role as a human resource manager. But her actions and thoughts were contradicting her goal. During her conversation with me, she kept repeating to me how she wanted her boss to change her views and trust this lady by delegating more work to her. You see the difference here? I want you to get to the root of this. Her desire was, "I want to get more independent in my role as a human resources manager." Her thoughts were, "I want my boss to change and to realize that she can trust me with more work." Her actions will now be completely at odds with her goal. Rather than focusing on how she could get better at her job and build a confident relationship with her boss, she will focus on how her boss must change. Most of us make this mistake unconsciously every day at our workplace. We must know that we've got to lead the change ourselves. It begins by first changing our thoughts. Your thoughts attract your situation to you. Your boss, your business, your clients, your team, and all are attracted to you by the way you think.

A friend of mine always told me that her husband wasn't too ambitious. He was never in a hurry to climb the corporate ladder and preferred a relaxed job atmosphere with the least pressure. When I met him at a dinner party, I enquired about his job and how he felt about it. He said he was stress free and glad to be working away from the head office in San Jose, California. However, he wasn't satisfied with his boss and team. He felt that his boss did not push people enough to achieve more and that his team appeared too relaxed. He wanted to be part of a winning team. Do you see the difference again? He wanted to be part of a winning team but also preferred a relaxed work life. We get what we think.

I want you to reflect on this question. How many times do you think and talk in ways that take you away from your goals and dreams? We all want to lead a healthy life, and yet we go through life eating processed fast food because it's easy, convenient, and cheap. And we all know its effects on our health. You want to share your ideas at work and be the person who can lead, but then you fade into the corner of the meeting room with no curiosity, no clarity, and nothing bold to express. You quietly let the world and the work pass you by. Your current situation and the people around you are there for a reason. And that reason is you. Until you change, nothing changes. Begin to lead the change. Let this equation help you:

$$\text{Unstoppable Success} = (\text{Picture} + \text{Thoughts}) \times \text{Action}$$

This equation means that for you to achieve unstoppable success, you've got to make your thoughts and the picture go together. What we picture and think about it determine our actions. Your personal *picture* of reality is determined by the thoughts you hold. So if you picture yourself with more income, better position, more business, and better clients, then your thoughts should be about abundance, not scarcity. Together, picture plus thoughts is now multiplied with actions. When picture and thoughts are aligned, you will be able to take big actions without fear. People will want to follow you. You will be an influencer. Your business will grow, and your work will create a lasting impact. If you want your circumstances, your results, and your life to change for the better, then know that success demands fluidity, which requires you as a leader to be willing to make a change to the state of your inner leader.

The Leader's Role in Organizational Culture

Does the leader create the culture or does the culture create the leader? You may have heard this question before—what came first, the chicken or the egg? When organizations engage *Success Is Within Leadership* for an employee workshop, I ask my audience—does the leader create the culture or does culture create the leader? I believe one can have the most well-thought-through strategy, but if you don't have a culture to support it, you're doomed. I also believe that your competitor can copy everything about your organizations except its deeply rooted culture. Most companies craft great values while articulating their organization's culture. But they forget that it's the people who carry out the culture and make it a success. The leader creates the culture, *and* culture creates the leader. They go hand in hand. Habits and rituals of your people make up the pace and cadence of your organization. Do your people have a habit of winning? Do your people act like a success each day? What is their thinking during times of change and uncertainty? When you examine these aspects of your people, you can find clues about whether they are going to embrace change with flexibility or seize up with resistance and break apart. That in turn will help you redefine your company culture. I have been helping people and organizations create a culture where people act like a success, and develop a culture of leadership and success. This one element has a direct correlation with your bottom line. It is enough to keep you ahead in the game.

For years, I wondered why I kept getting clients who weren't able to pay me well? Why did I end up speaking at places where there was no monetary value? Why was I getting jobs where all the time I was the one who suffered? Well, it became clear to me that evening as I cried in the closet, that everything was happening for one reason, and that reason was me. There was a huge difference between my desires and my thinking. I had crafted perfect plans and strategies, but I hadn't developed a powerful mindset to convert my ideas into actions. I hadn't developed the execution mindset, something I teach people today. I knew then that I had to lead the change that I wanted to see. And as I got enlightened that the root was me, I began to change the reality by applying this one mantra each day in my life: the mantra of acting like a success.

Since that day when I changed myself, I have taught this mantra to millions of people and organizations, and they have seen the results. The reason I crafted this mantra is because in my two decades of work with companies small and large, I have observed at root that a significant 65% of a company's market value is attributable to how its people and leaders behave and that this plays a key role in shaping a company's reputation. Leaders have a powerful influence on an organization's culture. They set the tone for how people perceive their work experience. How they act defines the work culture. I once spoke to the leadership team of an amazing company in South Korea. The chairman of this company always tells his people that everyone is CEO of their department, and their contribution is imperative to overall company growth. This inspires his people to take ownership of their areas of responsibility as a CEO would. Do your people act as CEOs or as employees? You may have set the vision, the values, and the core desired behaviors that are imperative to steer the organization towards excellence. But until every person in your organization *exhibits* the required behavior, the culture and results will be impacted negatively. People must be willing to step into their greatness and give their best. But there is a reason why most do not. People I meet often ask me, "Payal, how did you do it? How did you go from surviving to thriving in your work life?" I often answered briefly by talking about focus and passion. But when I sought to recount the process of what it took to transform my life into something prosperous and compelling, the best answer came from my daughter's high school psychology textbook. She was reading about "relative deprivation," and as I explained the concept to her, it gave me answers to many of my own problems.

Have you ever felt that you have less than what you deserve in life? That your coworker or competitor is doing much better than you despite your efforts? Let's say you bought a beautiful white luxury Lexus, and you were proud of it until you saw that your coworker, while getting the same salary as you, drives a fancier Tesla. How do you feel about your car now? If it changes your feelings, you are experiencing relative deprivation. In simple terms, relative deprivation is a feeling that you are generally "worse off" or "not as well off" as the people you associate with. And let me tell you, we all experience this—sometimes just at mild annoyance level but many times more strongly. And when we allow this experience to strongly affect your emotions, it begins to drag us down. We look at people's success and wish we could get that overnight success too. Believe me, there is no overnight success. I've worked with numerous successful people in the world, and I have witnessed firsthand that success is often a slow process, one day, one step at a time. I used to get caught in relative deprivation syndrome, where I would compare myself to others who are super successful in their careers, and I would tell myself, "I want to be where they are." This feeling of wanting instant success and experiencing strong bouts of relative deprivation is devastating to your self-esteem and progress. There is a difference, though, between looking up to someone as a role model and comparing yourself to someone. Comparison causes you to neglect your real goals and to take the wrong decisions in your life based on another person's path. You begin to change your goal in the face of that comparison and find yourself on *their* path now instead of your own. Instead, use your energy to perfect *your* game, not someone else's. Many of you are afraid to step into your success because you're too busy comparing yourself to someone else. You *are* unique and can make a difference. Begin to act like a success. When you and everyone around you begin to act like successes, together there is huge power that steers your destiny and that of your organization towards growth. When you act like a success, you create your reality.

The Power of an Illusion

A businessman was in debt and couldn't figure a way out of it. Creditors were pressing him. Suppliers were demanding payment. He was sitting on a bench in the park with his head down, desperately thinking about what could save the company from bankruptcy. Suddenly, an old man appeared in front of him.

"I see that something is bothering you," he said. After listening to the businessman's woes, the old man said, "I think I can help you." He asked the businessman what his name was, wrote him a check, and said "Take this money. We will meet here exactly in one year, and you will be able to return it to me at that time." Then, he turned around and disappeared just as suddenly as he had appeared.

The businessman saw that he had a check in his hands for five hundred thousand dollars, signed by John Rockefeller, one of the richest people in the world at that time!

"I could end all of my problems in no time!" He exclaimed to himself. But instead, the businessman decided to put the check into his safe. Just the thought of its existence gave him strength to find a solution to save his business. With the return of his optimism, he concluded profitable deals. Within a couple of months, he got out of debt and started to earn money again.

Exactly one year later, he returned to the park with the same check in hand. At the agreed time, the old man appeared again. At the moment when the businessman wanted to return the check and to share his story of success, a nurse suddenly ran up and grabbed the old man.

"I'm so glad, I caught him!" she exclaimed. "I hope he wasn't bothering you. He always runs away from the house and tells people he is John Rockefeller."

The businessman smiled in surprise. During that whole year, he had been rebuilding his business, buying and selling, convinced that he had half a million dollars. Suddenly, he understood that it's not the money, real or imaginary, that turned his life around. It was his new confidence and inner belief that gave him strength to achieve everything that he had now.

A man who had lost all hope and was on the verge of committing suicide was able to change his destiny? What made him do that? Was it the check or was it his mindset? Of course, it was his own mindset that changed his destiny. How many people in the world do you know who have the best of everything and yet are struggling? You and I both know stories of rags to riches too. The reason this man succeeded was because when he changed his mindset, he began acting like a success.

Most of us do *not* act like a success. We think and act as failures, as average, and as victims. Your time, your efforts, and your career are too valuable to squander on just being average. Average feels safe, but it's not. Average people are the first to get kicked on their butts. The average zone is a place where you are invisible, lost among the millions of anonymous people who go to work each day. You definitely deserve better than the average. Acting like a success changes the entire game for you and for your organization. It's a powerful mantra that is mostly ignored today in leadership. Instead of waiting to see how things turn out, hoping that they will get better, or simply allowing the circumstances and situations in your life to determine how you feel, you can act like a success, knowing fully well that success is already within you. Everything that you need to be successful, happy, and fulfilled is within you and around you. Now you might be saying to yourself, "how can I act like a success when the reality is that I am not. Is this not a lie I tell myself?" Well, acting like a success is not the same as *fake it till you make it*. So, the answer to your question is no, you are not lying to yourself. In fact, you are speaking utmost truth; the truth which is your reality. Think deeply about this question: "Do thoughts create your reality or does the reality create your thoughts?"

Say for example you are facing a conflict with your boss. This is your reality, no doubt about it. Now, this reality can create a thought that "Oh, my boss is terrible. He makes my life at work miserable." When someone asks you how you are doing at work, you tell them the same thing: "Oh, my boss is terrible. He makes my work life miserable. I am so sick of it. I feel terrible." And then imagine that you repeat this sentiment for the entire day. Soon this attitude will enter your subconscious mind, and symptoms will begin to appear in your actions. You will surely begin to hate the very name and sight of your boss. Your relationship with your boss with be negatively impacted. Your performance will drop significantly. Most of the time you will be either complaining or looking out for a new job. You will not be giving your best, and your results will be poor. Your reality created a new thought which in turn manifested a new reality. Contrary to this scenario, if your thoughts are something like, "My relationship with my boss is getting better. I understand where he comes from," and you repeat this thought the entire day, how will you begin to feel? Soon this will enter your subconscious mind, and symptoms will appear in your actions. You will surely begin to work things out between you and your boss. Your relationship with your boss will begin to improve. Your performance at work will be better. You will try to see where the loopholes are so you can fill them up while you are still there. You will pay more attention to your projects and take responsibility for delivering great results. Your thought has brought you to a new reality of well-being. Soon this begins to align with the organization's culture, making it deeper and stronger. Isn't this exactly what you wished for? Is this not aligning with your success? So acting like a success is not about faking it or it giving you miraculous results without any effort. Although the process appears simple, it is hard to practice. That is why most people do not attempt it. It's hard to act like a success when you are struggling to make ends meet. If you do build the courage to act like a success, though, I assure you that you're going to feel a new confidence level, a new boldness to step into your destiny. You will begin to break the chain of inferiority that is holding you back. You will begin to experience unstoppable success in your job and business. Is it not rightly said that you become what you believe you are?

I know that it does seem difficult to imagine that our most happy, sad, and other emotional moments in life are nothing more than an illusion created in our minds. Even more surprising is the suggestion that everyone can create the reality they choose. How is it possible? It's based on quantum physics, neuroscience, and cognitive neuro-engineering, all of which simply state that everything and everyone is made up of atoms, and atoms carry energy vibrating at a certain frequency, and they tend to come in contact with other atoms vibrating at the same frequency. In fact, Shankari Rajangam, a neuroscientist at Duke University, has this to say regarding how mental imagery practice is a proven technique in learning a new skill such as playing a musical instrument or a new sport:

> Mental practice done by replaying the movement sequence in the head complements physical training done by athletes and musicians and helps to improve performance. Brain rewiring, also referred to as neural plasticity, occurs with learning and repetition of any task, physical or mental. It is more interesting if we delve deeper and look at what underlies the changes that occur with practice and repetition. At the single neuron level new connections are formed and pruned with repeated practice. New memories and learning new skills happen at this cellular level wherein repeated stimulation strengthens neuronal connections at the synapse. Repetition alters synaptic efficacy that outlasts the initial stimulation forming cellular memories. So beware of what you repeat mentally and physically.

I would like to add here that everything starts with a thought. Look around you. Everything you see in our physical world started as an idea. Our thoughts have created the light bulb, the train, the airplane, the TV, the car, the rocket, and the robot. They all were once thoughts in someone's mind. Uber was a thought and so was Tesla. Computers were once a thought and so were memory materials. Everything you perceive in the physical world has its origin in the invisible, inner world of your thoughts. Acting like a success is based on the concept of *Success Is Within* that says humans can create their own reality with the power of their thinking. Wayne Dyer wrote a great book a number of years ago called *You'll See It When You Believe It*. So many of us, myself included, have lived important phases of our lives with the silent mantra of "I'll believe it when I see it." and in doing so we hold ourselves back, limit what's possible, and negate the power of our mind to allow and create things, situations, experiences, and outcomes that are new, unpredictable, and even miraculous.

Let's try and challenge our limiting thought through this simple exercise called the rapid priming method (RPM). If you want more out of your life, you must recognize your limiting thoughts and know how to change them to your advantage. RPM helps you reframe and reshape your limiting thoughts within five minutes so you can take actions towards your dreams.

Step 1: Identify your limiting thought, e.g., "Not everyone can make it to the top of an organization."

Step 2: Document evidences that backs up your limiting thought.

Step 3: To change your thought, look for the generalizations and check to see what is missing—essentially create doubt in your limiting thought.

Step 4: Create a new empowered thought.

Choose Your Reality

When you were born, the universe created a unique masterpiece. You're the right size, the right color, the right nationality with all the right gifts in the right environment. It programmed you to be successful and victorious. It programmed you for mastery and not victimhood. Then, what stands between you and success? We do not choose our reality. There is a myriad of options available to us these days. We are in an age of what I call "over-choices." Making a decision becomes overwhelming because there is so much to choose from. We want everything. Consider you're sitting at your office desk, working on a project. You're suddenly struck with the desire to do something different. You rise to your feet and are suddenly dealing with a decision among infinite options of reality: you could go to the restroom; you could go to the meeting room; you could walk outside; you could grab your phone and chat, you could go over to a colleague and talk, you could make a call home, you could get on a website and enroll in a class, you could call a potential client, you could drive down to a KFC and eat, or you could walk out of your job. The point is you could do nearly *anything* you can imagine. This is the power you have in every moment: to pull yourself consciously into the one reality that seems most in line with your desired outcome. And whichever reality you do choose to manifest, then you've collapsed all other possibilities.

This is what David did. At one time, David found himself stuck in a dead end job. His boss was a disaster, and David was unhappy. He rose to his feet and then emailed his boss and boss's boss for a meeting. He explained his problem and how he wanted to continue. He proposed an alternative that they not only liked but that moved him with a promotion to another unit. David was super happy. David chose to manifest a reality of giving it a try and collapsed all other realities like quitting, blaming, or sticking around unhappy. My question to you is, "What reality do you want to create for yourself?" Can you fill in this blank? "I want to _____." If you want to create a reality of having many clients in your business, then collapse all other realities of enjoying television, having a relaxed life, socializing, and spending time on social media. If you want to create a reality of becoming a doctor, author, hair stylist, director, or CEO, then make sure you collapse all other realities that take you away from what you desire. This is because you can create and think only one reality at a time. And once you have created your reality, you are already a success. Think deeply about this; to be successful at anything in your life, what is the very first thing you've got to do? You've got to be clear on what you want. No matter what is going on in your work life today, I urge you to take the very first and most crucial step for your success. Choose your reality. Be honest about this. Look at your present circumstances, and know that you chose this reality and collapsed all the other possibilities. Whenever you are stuck and don't know the way to go, just step back and choose a reality you want to connect to. I feel certain you will see a definite connection. So true are the lines, "Let your eyes look straight ahead (on your reality), and let your gaze be straight before you" (Proverbs 4:25). Now, once you've created this goal or reality, think about how successful people act. Or may I say, how would you act like a success? If you act as if you're already where you want to be, the universe will respond to those vibrations. A magician, after attending my leadership workshop, asked himself, "If I were already a world-famous magician, how would I act?"

As a successful person, you would be moving around with a ferocious focus, a confident way of walking, a mind full of ideas, the courage to speak up at meetings, the urge and determination to solve problems, the excitement to learn something new each day, the passion to innovate, and be more committed than ever. That's it. You are acting like a success. So if you want to become an entrepreneur, a director, a CEO, and a best-seller author, I challenge you today, from this moment on, begin to act like a success. You will be amazed at the change this brings to your energy level, your thought process, your actions, and your final outcome.

Take a look at the table below. I want you to read every statement from both columns and mark at least three asterisks in total on statements that resonate with you. Then, check if the asterisks weigh more towards acting more like a failure or acting like a success. Once you know what direction you tilt more towards, use the miraculous practice called thought traffic control (TTC) to shift from acting like a failure to acting like a success. And if you are already acting like a success, it is bound to help you stay there longer. TTC has proven to help people increase their productivity, to be more innovative and deliver best results.

Acting Like a Failure	Acting Like a Success
If only I had more ... (Feeling of lack)	Let's see what I have with me (Feeling of abundance)
I will do this when ... (Procrastinating)	I will start now (Action)
It's all because of ... (Blaming)	I should've paid more attention to it (Responsibility)
Success is destined for the lucky few (Assumptions)	Success is within (Belief)
It's too hard to work on this (Quitting)	Let me see how this can be done (Trying)
They are so lucky (Envying)	I am lucky (Satisfaction)
I'll see what's on social media (Time wasting)	Let me see what's new I can learn (Time investing)
Job is horrible and stressful (Complaining)	Thank goodness I have a job in these times (Grateful)
It's not going to happen (Hoping for failure)	It's possible (Hoping for success)
There are so many problems (Focusing on the wrong things)	There are so many possibilities (Focusing on the right things)
No one has ever done this, it can't be done (Dreaming small)	No one has ever done this, it can be a new opportunity (Dreaming big)
Worried about tomorrow (No hope)	Prepared for tomorrow (Hopeful)
Work is stressful (Negative perspective)	Work is enjoyable (Positive perspective)

Thought Traffic Control (TTC)

How many times have you said to yourself or heard someone say, "I feel like I'm losing my mind." This is because you are unable to control the traffic of thoughts running through your mind. The traffic of thoughts seems to kidnap your mind. Have you ever seen or been in a traffic jam? How does that feel? Does it make you feel stressed, irritated, impatient, and helpless? The situation of our mind is similar. Throughout the day thoughts flow in and out, and soon there is a traffic jam inside of you that does not allow you to think clearly and move through your situation. Now, just like you cannot control the flow of a river, similarly you cannot control the flow of your thoughts. But you can control the traffic jam it creates within you. Similar to how you take tea and coffee breaks in a day, or get up from your chair every hour to stretch, take a break every hour for a minute to control the traffic of thoughts. Give them a break too. In this break time, free your mind of uncontrolled mental chatter. Just pause for a minute and check the quality of your thoughts, along with the resultant feelings and/or actions in the hour gone by. Then, commit to an empowered thought for the next hour. Repeat the same after another hour. This will bring down the level of stressful thoughts and create space for empowering thoughts. By the end of the day, you will be amazed at how high your energy level remains despite work pressure and any other circumstances you may have encountered throughout the day. Soon your mind will automatically start resisting the ideas of giving up, making impulsive decisions, getting angry, or reacting adversely. When you do this repeatedly, the wiring in your brain changes from a habitual reaction to empowering response.

I believe as you act so you attract. All things that are happening to you and around you are based on your energy and its vibration frequency. You send out a frequency, and it attracts someone or a situation of the same frequency. Someone said, "Our life is simply a reflection of our actions. Life will give you back everything you have given to it." I believe today is going to be the start of a transformation in your life. Stop looking at where you are and focus on where you want to be. Think your way to being successful. If you allow your mind to go there, your actions will follow your thinking. When you repeat the mantra below daily, you will witness a huge change in your actions. You will be more responsible towards your actions because you know they will create your reality today.

Mantra: "If I can dream it, I can act like it."

MANTRA 3

Perform Actions

In today's volatile business climate, all companies are facing similar challenges: how do we stay competitive in a complex and volatile business environment? How do we drive breakthrough innovation with increasingly limited resources? For many years now, I have been strategically inspiring people to convert their thinking and ideas into desirable actions. Action is a significant element today for unstoppable success. The huge gap between average and exceptional leaders, and between the "successful few" and the "unsuccessful many" is because of action. Many of us are experts at articulating our goals. Time and again we leaders have been drilled with the importance of having a clear goal. Corporations have spent millions of dollars training their employees on how to set and achieve goals. Yet how many of us achieve one goal after another with speed and serenity? During my workshops and coaching sessions, I ask my participants to write one goal that they truly want to achieve in their career and business. When I see them thinking about that goal, and then writing and rewriting it, it reminds me of a story about fifty tiny of frogs in a jungle.

In this story, the frogs arrange a competition to reach the top of the highest tower in town. As the date for the competition is announced, the news spreads, and large crowds gather around the tower to cheer the contestants. The frogs are determined to achieve their goals and are full of potential and belief.

The crowd does not believe that these little frogs are going to make it to the top of the tower, yet they are curious. The competition begins, the frogs quickly begin to ascend the tower, and the crowd cheers!

After a few moments, someone from the crowd shouts, "There's no chance that they will succeed. The tower is too high!"

Another spectator adds, "They will never make it to the top. It's way too difficult!"

As the competition continues, the tiny frogs collapse, one by one, tired and exhausted. The race continues, and the remaining frogs passionately climb higher and higher.

In the excitement and anxiety, the crowd continues to yell, "It's too difficult. No one will make it!" More tiny frogs get tired and gave up. They all continued to give up one by one, until there is only ONE little frog left in the competition who continues to climb higher and higher and higher ....

This one wouldn't give up!

This one tiny frog who, after a big effort from all the others is the only one who reaches the top! This little soul is the winner! He made it! He got the glory!

Naturally, everyone wants to know how this one tiny frog managed to pull it off when every other contestant gave up. Everybody wants to know how this tiny frog found the strength to reach this goal that everyone else thought was impossible. So, they ask questions.

It turned out that the winner is deaf.

The story highlights an important fact of life that when it comes to your goals and dreams, all that matters is moving ahead and being unstoppable. Let me bring your attention to some numbers. In the story, there are fifty frogs, each of whom made a goal to reach to the top. Only one frog made it to the top. In the world of humans, millions of people make goals. And we know how small of a percentage achieve them. So, do you see yourself as a person full of mind-blowing ideas, but find it hard to achieve them? And then do you begin a process of blaming your boss, teams, clients, friends, economy, and even the weather for your failures and disappointments? Do you start to give up on your goals and dreams? With this attitude, you will remain stuck in the same role for years, and growth in your job and business will begin to slow down. A quote I often return to is, "the most dangerous place on earth to live is your comfort zone, and the wealthiest place on earth is the graveyard. In both places you will find unfulfilled dreams, goals and hopes, because someone did not execute them and did not take any actions." It all comes down to taking action. In the process of walking towards your dream and purpose, you're going to encounter many challenges; you are going to face a lot of failures, hardships, tears, and rejections. Not everyone will stand with you in your pursuit of your dreams, but that's not important. What matters most is whether you are willing to stand up for your dreams and goals. Are you willing to rise above all the negativity around you? Are you willing to instruct your mind not to give up? Are you willing to push yourself to deliver the best each day regardless of the situation at your workplace? If your answer is yes, then commit and make a pledge to yourself today that you will to take actions.

The Action Pledge below helps people to progress, and many have created empires that you see standing strong today. It has helped people expand their business. It has helped people to get unstuck and move ahead. It has inspired youth to take steps ahead in their lives. So with full faith in yourself and in the universe, repeat this pledge every day, many times a day, and begin to experience success. The Action Pledge will not change your results immediately, but it will never let your potential lie dormant. It will open up your mind to ideas and show you the next step towards progress. It will begin to change your state from depression to a feeling of exuberance. It will pump you with energy to take your actions. And that's the first step to beginning to change your results.

The Action Pledge

When obstacles arise and life seems like a mountain, I will take my action and cross over. When fear grips and pulls me into the darkness, I will push myself to take action. When worry strikes me and anxiety takes over, I will take action and carve my path. And when I achieve my goal, I will not rest, but will take more actions to create my destiny of choice.

Reaching for the Power to Take Action

Like the frog in my earlier story, you want to remain deaf to all the negativity around you; you cannot curse or change the system or other people. You've got to stay in the system, you've got to navigate through all the politics and challenges, and you've got to reach your goal. If there is one thing that you can do all the time, it's to perform your actions. You have a right to your actions. Be determined to take your actions regardless of the challenges. Action is at the fundamental core of leadership and success. It is what distinguishes an average leader from exceptional leaders. Yet, most of us cannot seem to grasp this concept completely. Your every result and your every relationship are based on your actions. But most of the time we forget about our actions and focus more on what other people's actions might be. One of my coaching clients, Anita, an aspiring business woman, ran wisdom coaching classes for youth. Her dream was to expand her business and spread this wisdom to youth across the world. She had goals, she had plans, but she missed the actions step. She wanted to reach out to major organizations and corporations but limited herself because she always said to herself, "companies aren't going to respond to me." She wanted to develop online classes to reach mass people and often said, "I don't think many people will join in." Because of this attitude, she remained like the forty-nine frogs who gave up. She was constantly focused on what the other person's action would be. That tempted her to give up often on her ideas because 90% of the time we think the other person's action towards us to be negative.

But today, after coaching from me, she is able to strategically execute her ideas and spread her work across five countries while still expanding her reach. When you have not listed and taken your actions, you are more likely to doubt yourself and to believe people around you who tell you it's impossible. I challenge you to pause in your reading right now and list your main goal for the next three months. Then, list below it all the potential actions you must take to reach your goal. Don't limit your action listing based on whether it's possible or not. Write out a half-dozen small actions, some seemingly insignificant and others potentially significant that you can do every day to go a different direction. Keep that list with you until we reach the end of this chapter.

Many years back, I was one among the forty-nine frogs. I would listen to what people had to say, I would keep thinking of what reaction my action would get, and then I allowed that to stop me from unleashing my potential. Every time my father would talk to me about ideas and ways of moving ahead in my job, and share some action for me to take, I would reply to him with something like this: "They will not return my call," or "I don't think they will connect me to the CEO," or "What's the use of taking action when I know what the results will be?" My dad seems to have caught my pattern of thought, and one fine day he sat me down, took a sheet of paper, and said,

Payal, far off in the jungles of Africa, every morning with the first rays of the sun a lion wakes up and runs faster than the fastest deer in the jungle. In the same jungle every morning with the first rays of the sun a deer wakes up and runs faster than the fastest lion in the jungle. Each of them has a goal—the lion must satisfy his hunger, and the deer must safeguard its life. If the lion were to think, "What's the point of running, the deer is so fast that I can barely catch it?" then the lion would die of hunger. If the deer were to think, "I know the lion will eventually catch me, so why run?" then the deer would lose its precious life. This is what you are doing Payal. You have the potential, you have the ideas, but you tend to think of the actions of the others in response to your action, and that's why you fail to take massive actions which show up in your results.

He then wrote the following equation on paper, which has continued to help me and all of my clients to understand the power of one's actions. Here is the equation and what he explained to me that became one of the most important lessons in my leadership journey:

Ad hoc Success = 50% of your action +

50% expected action of others

Success is a combination of 50% your action and 50% the action another might take, which we call their response to your action. You are in control of only your 50% share. You have a right to make your share of action 100% or 25%. When you keep thinking negatively of the response you might get to your actions, your energy and motivation will reduce and you will reduce your share of action. When you fully concentrate on your actions and think of all the ways you can move ahead giving your best regardless of the response from the other end, your energy level and motivation will reach its peak, and you will increase your share of action to 100%. Now the equation changes:

Unstoppable Success = 100% of your unstoppable action +

0% expectation of others' action

This equation means that regardless of whether the other person takes action or not, you are willing to at all the time take 100% action. It means that if you do happen to get a positive response from the other side, you get positive results, and if not, you definitely have the satisfaction of doing your part to the best of your capability, learning what worked and what didn't and deciding on your next action. You are willing to do your part. You are committed to unstoppable action. You become like that lion who wakes up and hunts every morning. You give your best regardless of the economy or people's behavior. Leadership is action, not position. Often, the action comes first; the title second.

Being able to execute means having the ability to get the job done. Being able to execute is a unique and distinct mindset. It means you know how to put decisions into action and push them forward to completion. Ask yourself: Do I continually drive results both personally and for my organization? Mother Teresa said, "If each of us would only sweep our own doorstep, the whole world would be clean."

Michelle's Story

One afternoon while having a business lunch with one of my good friends and associates, Michelle Proctor, who is the Chief of Staff of the Risk Division at SAS Institute and a successful woman in STEM, I asked her what her message would be to people who aspire to become exceptional leaders and achieve success. "My advice to the up-and-comer," she said, "is to have a positive attitude and be the person who's efficient with their time. Raise your hand to take on the extra assignments that make a difference to the organization. Be the person who goes above and beyond without being asked, and I promise, you will reap the benefits!" Michelle says she draws on this thought from her own childhood lesson in life:

> I grew up embracing the concept of servant leadership without even knowing what it was. Now that I have more than twenty years of experience, ranging from a short stint as an individual contributor to a team lead and manager and now in upper management, I've had the honor and privilege of mentoring lots of individuals along the way. I often get asked by my mentees what they can do to differentiate themselves in a way that will get them noticed in order to advance in their careers. I can't help but draw a parallel to the simple advice my father gave me at the age of ten when I was leaving for my very first babysitting gig. It was for our next-door neighbor who was paying me twenty-five cents an hour to watch her toddler while she did outside chores

around the house. Quite simply, he told me that as an employer, my neighbor had a choice as to who she hired to spend time with her child. He went on to explain that it is not only important to play with the child and get along with her well (i.e., do the job I was hired to do). In addition to that, say, while the baby was napping, if I took the time to clean the kitchen or straighten up the livingroom while the parents were away, then I would likely become the person they tried to hire first any time they needed a sitter.

I used this strategy and was booked almost every weekend for years. Soon my parents were borrowing petty cash from me in between their trips to the bank! While this seems like a little childhood story, the true lesson in leadership lies in understanding that employers also have the choice in who gets the reward and recognition. They have the ability to differentiate employees silently in a way that matters. Managers notice the employee who finishes their own work then looks up to find the next thing in the organization they can help without being asked. The rare jewel in the organization notices a need and proactively works on a solution. The one who brings forward a prototype or a plan to achieve resolution, is indeed the true hero that rises to the top. These are the individuals who receive larger bonuses, are given the awards and stock options. They are promoted beyond their peers and more quickly. These individuals are granted that extra percent or two when pay increases come around.

My thoughts resonate deeply with what Michelle says. It has always been my own belief that one needs to create a personal differentiation in this crowded market. You've got to go beyond your job description and set goals to deliver the best. Don't let the fear of failure limit your action and potential. Let it not define who you are. In one of his interviews, I remember how Jack Welch, former chairman and CEO of General Electric, saw every challenge or task as an opportunity to get out of the pile and differentiate himself. He knew that just answering what he was asked to do would not get him anything.

Action and Execution

Achieving unstoppable success is about your execution of ideas. It's about all the actions you are willing to take. It needs discipline. Many times I have observed people and organizations blame lack of strategy when execution fails. Strategy is simply the art of planning. Execution is all about the discipline to translate your big ideas into concrete, doable actions. No company and no individual can deliver on its promises or overdeliver without taking action. Execution is everybody's responsibility. Begin to make it the core of your being and of your organization's culture. This is the only way you will increase accountability. Immerse yourself in taking actions daily. Many deals are lost because of lack of action. You've got to go beyond and take as many actions as you can in the direction of your goal.

In one of the conferences I gave at the Raleigh Convention Center in North Carolina, I saw a familiar face in the audience. I noticed she recognized me but shied away from meeting with me. After the conference was over, I went up to her, greeted her, and talked to her. I observed she was low in confidence. She spoke about her work, and soon we were talking about how she could be successful at her job and climb the corporate ladder. I shared with her a couple of techniques that she could possibly use, and she loved them. She set up an appointment with me, and soon I was coaching her. The equation for this action remains the same:

Unstoppable success = 100% your unstoppable action +

0% expectation of others' action

If I were to think on the lines of, "Why should I approach her?" or "I don't think she is interested in speaking with me," then I would not only have lost a coaching relationship contract but also have lost connecting to more great leaders she helped me connect with from her company.

In yet another case, I got to interact with a taxi driver who drove me from my hotel in Cape Town to where I was to deliver a keynote. The distance was only about thirty minutes when there was no traffic. I must tell you those thirty minutes went by so quickly with her. As this taxi driver greeted me and I became comfortable, she asked me what I did for a living. I told her I was a motivational leadership speaker, executive and success coach, and an author. She was excited on hearing my role and shared how she wanted to be a great leader in her work. I got to know during our conversation that she was an insurance agent and that she drove a taxi to support her business. We exchanged many notes, and finally, when I was leaving the taxi, she also handed me her insurance business card and asked me, "Is there anyone whom you know that could benefit from purchasing insurance from me?" I told her I would pass on her reference, which eventually I. And some of those I recommended to her did connect with her. She had taken 100% of her action without thinking if I would recommend her or not. The same equation applies:

Unstoppable success = 100% of your action +

0% expectation of others' action

How many times in your life have you decided not to ask somebody for something (inaction), assuming that the other person would not be interested? How many times have you avoided taking action which you knew you must take? There is always the chance, however small, that the person will accept your offer, but you've killed that opportunity by not making the "ask" (your action). You've already negotiated with yourself and decided that the answer would be "No!" Never negotiate with yourself. If Steve Jobs had negotiated only with himself, Apple Computer would probably not have been created. Despite all the importance of action, most people shy away from it. The main reason for this shyness seems to be fear of negative results, past experiences, and anxiety about the future. The "What if …?" grips people and pulls them back. "What if I fail? What if it's hard? What if I don't get the time? What if they reject me?!" And then we procrastinate. We don't feel like taking actions. *Two grains were lying side by side on fertile soil. The first grain said: "I want to grow up! I want to put down roots deep into the ground and sprout from the ground. I dream to blossom in delicate buds and proclaim the coming of spring. I want to feel the warm rays of sun and dew drops on my petals!" This grain grew up and became a beautiful flower. The second grain said: "I'm afraid. If I put down my roots into the ground, I don't know what they will face there. If I grow tender stems, they can be damaged by wind. If I grow flowers, they may be disrupted. So I'd rather wait for a safer time." Thus, the second grain waited until a chicken that passed by picked it up and gobbled it down.*

Just Begin

If you have your dream, do something with it. The first small action you take will make a great difference. If you just wait for the perfect conditions and keep worrying about what obstacles you may face, you'll end up doing nothing and soon you will be working to fulfill someone else's dream. The famous Indian poet Kabira said it best: "One who wants to get some pearls must dive deeply into the ocean. The person who fears drowning and sits at the shore will not get anything." I would like to add here a beautiful verse from the *Bhagavad Gita* (Chapter 3: Verse 8): "Perform your obligatory duty, because action is indeed better than inaction. Even the maintenance of your body would not be possible by inaction." This means action is inevitable. It is the most essential element of leadership. Even nature points us to the importance of action. Observe a stagnant pool and a running stream. Where water stagnates, it accumulates dirt and impurities. Whereas running water is clear and pure. If you are to succeed in life and be prosperous, follow the line of action. Be like the running stream. The river keeps moving, overcoming all obstacles. The universe responds to you, sooner or later, according to the quality of your actions.

Escaping the Procrastination Station

I have always been inspired by Nike's slogan: "Just do it." But how many of us "Just do it?" Look, the promise of being part of a new team, new project, new business deal, and new role fills us all with a rush that can never be duplicated. But after the so-called "passion" wears off, as challenges start to set in, and people start to leave you midway through; that is, when we begin to lose that spark, we begin to rethink about our goals and dreams, and start believing that it's impossible to achieve them. The result is procrastination. And even though today there are hundreds and thousands of books and products available to deal with procrastination, it really hasn't changed our results a whole lot. Research in an article in Inc.com pointed out that one out of five of us are chronic procrastinators. This is because most of us overestimate how much time we have left in our life. But not this Indian king I read about. He had a very special daily ritual. Every morning he was in the habit of celebrating his own funeral, complete with flowers and music all the while chanting, "I have lived fully, I have lived fully, I have lived fully." This leader knew one of the timeless secrets of leadership: live everyday as if it were your last.

How many of us can say that we have led a fulfilled work life? That we have given our best every single day? Too many people go to work as if they have an unlimited supply of time. They put off their dreams until another time. They promise to mend broken relationships, to expand their business, or deliver better results, but they continue to postpone their actions. Most people have big goals and dreams but lack only the action step to carry them through. This is why most people do not achieve success. Reading books, going to conferences, or listening to motivational tapes are all fantastic. But knowledge *must* be translated into action. Today, there's a very big gap between thinking and action. Consider all the time and money companies spend trying to improve their efficiency, or individuals spend trying to get into a better place in their life. Thinking and talking about problems rarely solves them, though.

Once you have identified the problem, identify the basic skills and resources necessary to build an action strategy to implement your goal. Leaders earn a track record for getting things done. What makes you successful is the execution of your ideas. Dreams don't work until you get up, put in the effort, and do the work. Have you seen how some people say they will do a hundred things but do not end up doing even one? And then, there are others who decide something in their mind and they are off to completing it right away. The difference between average leaders and exceptional leaders is in the quality and quantity of their actions. I've noticed that super successful people have continuously strived for actions that separate them from the rest. While most people are watching TV or sleeping, these successful few are taking actions towards their dream. Of course, I am not undermining the importance of family time. What I'm saying is that you are the sum total of your actions. The moment you commit yourself to go into your workplace each and every day as if it was your last, you undergo a profound part of the shift. The way you see your work changes fundamentally. You bring a new sense of energy and enthusiasm to your dreams and goals. You begin to feel inspired to give your best today. Each of us has a limited time in our career life. None of us know how, where, and when the end will arrive. The torch that you and I are holding today will be passed to future generations. Not everyone has the opportunity you and I have been given. If you were to travel and meet people like I do, you will see how many people around the world today are jobless. They want to earn money, but no one hires them. They wanted to make a difference at one point but were laid off from their company. They had the talent and wanted to expand their business but life ended up being short. If you are reading this book, you are fortunate to have been given the time by the universe to deliver. Give your best and take positive action each day.

The 1/1/1 Rule

In my presentations to companies, I introduce the concept of the "1/1/1 Action Rule." The rule simply says to focus on your 1% daily. As you focus on the 1% daily, it will have a compounding effect. The 1/1/1 rule has incredible power to change your life by changing your choices. Step by step, day by day, you will comprehend the incredible impact that small efforts can have on your life. This is how it works:

1 **Area:** Pick one area of your work life that you want to improve. Too often people want to improve many areas of their life at one time. But that's not what this strategy is about. In the current work environment we are in, there is an invisible force that is always trying to pull us in many directions. Instead of focusing on one thing at a time, we set multiple goals and think we can multitask ourselves to achieving them. A time-tested strategy that's been shared by many successful people is that you can achieve almost anything in life as long as you focus on achieving one thing at a time. Stick to one major priority per area of your work life. You can categorize your work life as follows: Income, time management, interpersonal communication, customer service, health, learning, growth, work life balance and relationships. Pick one from this category or add you own.

1 **Action:** Take a look at the list that you created earlier in this chapter where you listed all the actions you can take. Now mark an asterisk on just one action item. That one action is something you will immediately begin to implement in your daily life. However small the action may be, it's really important to begin to take action on that action. One action at a time can change your life. One action at a time can take you from average to great. Every day, commit to do something in relation to your goals. Have a daily action that needs to be completed and get them done, if you don't get them complete on that day take

it over to the next day, but make sure you make positive strides towards the life of your dreams, one action at a time.

1 Day: Make the best use of each day and every moment in your life. If you learn to master your today, you'll learn how to master your tomorrow and your life. All you need to do is become very, very good at living each day. When I shadowed executives to get to learn their patterns and routines, it was amazing how many of them worked each day with their thoughts fixed firmly in the past or in the future. They struggled to accept the realities of right here, right now. I concentrated on their daily routine. I believe that your daily routine speaks volumes about your thought pattern. How you think today tells me your results for tomorrow. There is no overnight success. Success is in what you do daily. Do you make a commitment to grow and be productive each day? Do you take the actions you have committed to take, regardless of your mood and circumstance each day? Your tomorrow can only be shaped by the things you do and the decisions you make every day. So today give your best. That's all there is to it. As Denise Brennan-Nelson said, "Someday is not a day of the week."

No matter what area of your life you want to improve—more money, more time, better relationships, higher productivity, or greater self-confidence, your actions will help you achieve all of your goals. Ultimately, you will be remembered not for your name, fame, or wealth, but for your actions, the ones you took and the ones you did not. Never shy away or become tired of taking actions. Take a deep look at this equation. Let it sink in, and remind yourself of it whenever inaction takes you over. This equation changed my way of thinking and brought about miraculous results for my clients too.

$$(1.00)^{365} = 1.00$$

$$(1.01)^{365} = 37.77$$

Each day of small consistent actions is bound to get you closer to your results than not taking any action. Never underestimate the power of actions however small they may be. If you do not commit to taking actions each day, your dreams will die, your goals will be left unaccomplished, and you will leave the earth feeling depressed and unfulfilled. Start to beat depression, overcome procrastination, surpass fear, and move ahead of failure with one leadership tool: actions. Begin to condition yourself to take productive actions daily. I remember Proverbs 12:11 in this context: "Those who work their land will have abundant food, but those who chase fantasies have no sense." Today, make a decision that you will revolutionize your results and your career by taking actions. Because today is the only day you have. Before you move ahead to reading the next mantra, answer this: Have you honestly put in the necessary work to achieve your goals?

Mantra: "The end is any moment, I must take my actions now."

MANTRA 4

Leaders Surrender

Finishing my full day Unstoppable Leadership Success workshop in Bangalore, India, I was heading back to my hotel in the taxi. On the way, I was making my notes from the session, and I remembered one term that everyone in the room wished to see attached to their teams, their bosses, and themselves. It was about "being fully engaged at work," which simply means putting everything you have into the company's goals, project at hand, and your own success. The more engaged you are at work, the more you'll get done. Basically, it's about performing at peak level every day and being immersed in your work. I thought to myself, "The market is full of tools and articles that can help in enhancing one's engagement at work. Then why is the problem of lack of employee engagement still persisting?" The taxi pulled in at the front door of my hotel, breaking my chain of thought. I gathered my belongings, paid the driver, and thanked him for his service. I went to my room to freshen up, and as I sat down to drink a hot cup of masala chai, the words "increase in productivity" still loomed over my mind. While sipping my hot masala chai, I began reading the newspaper and was captivated by the news about Hema Das. The article's bold heading read, "My focus is on the game, results come automatically." Hema Das is a young sprinter from the rice fields of Assam, India, who became a national hero *by winning the first-ever gold medal* in the IAAF World U-20 Championships in 2018. The heading reminded me of some words of wisdom shared by India's richest businessman,

Mukesh Ambani, in the business-standard magazine. He said, "If you focus on financial results, the chances are you will not become great and solve a problem." Taking another sip of my chai, I remembered what *actor Bryan Cranston* had written in his autobiography: "Ordinary people focus on the outcome. Extraordinary people focus on the process." In fact, many sports coaches like Morgan Wotten have reminded us to evaluate wins and losses objectively, focusing more on effort and execution than on the outcome of the game.

The Trap of Attachment to Results

I took a deep breath and concluded my thoughts on all of this with a quote from the *Bhagavad Gita*, one that I had often heard my father repeat: "You have a right to perform your prescribed duty, but you have no control over results. Never consider yourself to be the cause of the results of your activities and never be attached to not g your duty." In simple language, it means do not be attached to the results. Concentrate on your actions, and know that you are not the only cause of the results. Your results are influenced not only by your hard work but by many other unknown factors beyond your control. I put my cup of tea down to meditate further on this quote. I went back to the "productivity" problem and found a deep connection here. No company, small or large, no entrepreneur, and no individual can win over the long run without being fully engaged at their workplace. Only when people are fully engaged in their craft can there be increase in productivity. You cannot get to the highest level of your success without committing to being fully engaged in whatever you do. And this quote from the *Bhagavad Gita* gives a deeper answer to the problem of why lack of employee engagement persists despite all tools. This quote is the exact opposite of what we American business leaders are coached to do.

When I came to America twenty years ago, I heard people talk about the power of visualizing their outcomes. People focused heavily on their results and were doing everything to achieve those results. People spoke the language of outcomes. At one point, I began questioning myself; must I think or not think about the outcome? Don't results inspire us and motivate us to achieve more? My confusion was cleared when some years later I travelled to India on a work assignment. I still remember that evening when my dad and I went for a stroll to the nearby ice cream shop. As we each carried our ice cream and settled down on the benches outside the shop, my father excitedly asked me, "So, young lady, how's life in America?"

"Going great!" I replied. I chatted about my work and told him my goals and how I wanted to achieve them all. I told him about the American Dream and how through my work I wanted to live it. He could see my passion and enthusiasm. But he also saw something else that I didn't. He smiled, and asked me, "How would you feel if you were to achieve your dream?"

"I would feel so happy Dad, as if I were on top of the world," I said.

"OK," he replied. "And how would you feel if you were not to achieve these results, despite all your efforts?"

"Miserable!" "It would make me feel horrible, sad, and dejected. After all, look at the hard work and effort I am putting in."

OK. What would you do next?

I would keep pursuing until I got my result.

"In what condition, though?" he asked. I was confused and had no answer. My father continued in his deep voice. "Payal, how will you achieve your results when you are operating in a state of dejection and frustration, feeling miserable and sad? And even if you do continue, what would be the condition of your health and mind? Would you have enough stamina and enthusiasm to move on to the next and the next goal and be unstoppable? The answer is NO." He paused and took a deep breath as if troubled by his thoughts. He looked at me and asked, "Do you know why today there is so much tension, anxiety, stress, and sadness in the business world? Why despite all the benefits our workplace gives us we aren't happy at work? Why our work, which should be a sheer source of joy, has become a wellspring of tension? We aren't giving our best. We aren't fully engaged. It's because we are so deeply attached to results our condition is like that of these monkeys in Thailand":

> There were so many monkeys in this town that it started to cause problems to the local villagers and farmers. That's when a wise man stepped up and said to the community, "I've got a plan." He drilled a tiny hole on the side of a coconut and drained out the coconut water. The hole was big enough for a monkey's open hand to go through, but too small for a monkey's closed fist to go through. Then he filled a third of the coconut with peanuts and placed it near the trees that the monkeys frequently visited.
>
> One of the monkeys figured out that there were peanuts inside the coconut, so he stuck his tiny hand in there and grabbed a handful. When the villagers saw that they chased after the monkey. The monkey was now stressed, fearful, and panicked. He only had one free hand because the other hand was trapped in the coconut. The monkey would not let go of the peanuts. The monkey did not see that he could let go and free his other hand and climb away. He was eventually caught and killed by the villagers.

My father looked at me with a smile and said, "Sadly, this is our condition today. To achieve success, one needs to be hopeful, happy, passionate, healthy, confident, and enthusiastic. One also needs to have a calm mind and move with speed. Instead, we are full of worry, tension, stress, frustration, anxiety, unhappiness, ill health, and jealousy. If we get our results, it makes us happy, if we don't, we feel dejected. Your results are making you dance like a monkey, disturbing your state of mind constantly. One cannot deliver the best if one is affected by the results. Rather, our state of mind should be neutral and not a slave of outcomes. Remember, results are because of you, you are not because of the results. I challenge you to look into your life right now and see where you are still holding on to the peanuts, despite the fact that it may be harming your progress greatly and may hinder your successes and ultimate potential." I felt my ice cream melting away as he said these profound words. It made me think—how can we be detached from our results?

The Virtue of Detachment

As leaders, we are constantly reminded to achieve results. How can one remove oneself from all "personal" attachment to the outcome! Sounds counter-intuitive. After all, in business we are judged every day, every month, and every year by our numbers, and yes, we want results. I finally broke the silence and said, "Dad, everyone in the world focuses on the outcome. They are chasing their dreams. I fail to understand what's wrong with that." My dad understood that I had missed the finer points and the deeper meaning of the term *detachment*. He took time to explain this as we both walked back home. Taking me back to the story, he said,

> If only the monkey had detached himself from the peanuts (the results), he would have lived. The ability to let go, to surrender, to move on and not let the results influence you is essential for healthy living and for ultimate success. Humans should be able to avoid falling into such a trap. We should be able to understand the danger of holding on to things that don't serve us well. We should realize when we're creating traps for ourselves. Unfortunately, most of the traps in life are those we create for ourselves. We cling to the privilege of being right; we won't let go of anger and resentment; we become attached to material things that are of little value; and we often put our attachment to possessions and titles ahead of our own well-being.

No doubt, having goals and keeping an eye on the result is one of the most fundamental principles for success, but don't pursue the results directly. Focus on the process and on your actions with diligence, and let the outcome take care of itself. Think about it, an actor's only duty is to act. He or she must put in the best while acting. Whether the movie will be a block-buster or not is not in the actor's control. Besides their acting, the results depend on many other factors like the audience's perception, the movie direction and editing, the story line, the cinematography.

There are many things that play a role in the end result. However, if the movie did not go as expected and the actor takes himself to be the cause of the result, he will operate in a low state of mind. His mind will be cluttered with negative thoughts and he will sabotage himself. How do you think his performance will be in the next movie if his entire focus is on whether this next movie will be a blockbuster or not?

Similarly, no one can give their best performance at what-ever they do if part of their mind is preoccupied with the ten-sion and worry of the result. Productivity will fall short. You will be unable to make clear and right decisions. Ultimately the final results will be negative. That again brings you to a state of worry, tension, anxiety, and frustration, and you continue to operate in this manner. If you're going to find happiness and true success in life, you need to examine what you hold. Detach yourself from the results, never from your actions and duties. Great leaders surrender.

He concluded as we reached the front door of our home. Before enter-ing, my dad stopped, held my hand affectionately, and asked me, "Payal, I encourage and challenge you to take a close look at the attach-ments in your life. Do you place more importance on things outside of yourself than on things inside you? Does your goal and attachment to results get you into a monkey mind state? Are there things, when you surrender them, that will allow you to achieve your dream? Are you truly giving your best at your workplace? Realize that when you know your own inner qualities and strengths and have this awareness of surrendering in a conscious way, you are able to set yourself on an elevated position. No opposition, however powerful it may be, can shake you from your seat of self-respect." With these questions to reflect on, and the pearls of wisdom my father shared with me, I completed my assignment in India and headed back to America. These questions kept working on my mind each day.

The FME Pyramid for Extreme Productivity

With the passage of time, and in meeting successful and not so successful people, I was able to deconstruct the reason behind why few people are able to move from one goal to another with speed and serenity. Why some bounce back quickly from failures while others take ages. Why there is a culture of micromanagement in many companies, why people hop from one job to another, why success feels temporary, why material possessions and titles don't bring the happiness we crave. And most of all, I got the answer that solves the biggest problem that exists worldwide today at our workplaces—lack of productivity. One thing every single icon and elite performer I've watched has had in common is the ability to release their greatest productivity. I've taught people my proprietary system called the full-mind engagement (FME) pyramid to guide people to extreme productivity.

If you look at many of the most creative and productive people on the planet, they are working while engaging their minds completely on their task. While most people blame technology for distractions that hinder their productivity, I think distractions have always existed and will exist in the future too. You cannot blame technology for your lack of productivity. You've got to get to the root of the problem. I use the FME pyramid to help people break through and reach the peak of being fully engaged in their work, which leads them to extreme productivity. Take a look at the Figure 4.1, and note the different levels of

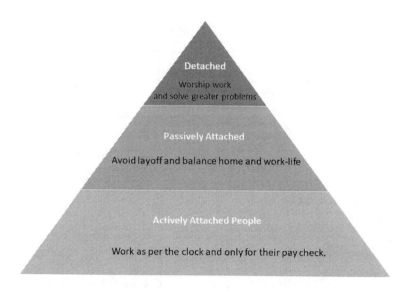

Figure 4.1   *The FME Pyramid for Extreme Productivity.*

mind distraction you and your people go through. They have nothing to do with technology yet they negatively affect one's productivity level.

At the bottom of the FME pyramid are people who are **actively attached**. These are people who have unknowingly attached themselves to their pride, doubts, old thinking patterns roles, teams, titles, ideas, negative beliefs, and in recent years to technology. For these people, everything revolves around "their" outcomes. If they don't see any growth, bonus, promotion, or high income, they will move on. Because they are attached to external factors, they are detached from the company itself. This means that at the very first opportunity, they will leave you for another company. These are the people who procrastinate often and miss deadlines. They are perpetually late for meetings. At this level, there is lack of learning, lack of challenge, and lack of motivation. They work as per the clock and only for their paycheck. These are people who are neither committed nor consistent. They don't take any pride in the company or its product and services. If you or anyone around you is operating at this level on the pyramid, remember that this lack of engagement at work is because these people have high levels of "personal" attachment, which brings with it higher potential for pain and sorrow. Why? Because when you are attached to something, you fear losing it. This fear sets off a chain reaction leading to negative behaviors. I have met plenty of leaders and entrepreneurs who succumbed to failure or stagnation in their work because of being actively attached to whatever they had gained until that point in their career life. Being actively attached can be a fatal blockage to experiencing unstoppable success. The deeper the attachment, the stronger the person is bound to the consequences of that attachment. I have met people who are attached to positions of great power. The power they have becomes an intoxicant for them. They cannot imagine their lives without it. Now let us imagine that in the business world, where everything is uncertain, if they were to lose their power, how would they feel? Let me tell you, they would be totally devastated over it. Attachment makes you vulnerable and insecure. It eats you up mentally from within and slows your progress. It does not let you think creatively because of fear.

In the middle of the pyramid are people who are **passively attached**. These are people who are proud to be where they are. They do their work diligently but aren't poised to put in extra effort. They have a great work record. They could be tempted and distracted towards other opportunities, though. They remain actively distracted by social media and technology. They complete the task as directed and do go beyond the average at times. But they have trouble staying on task. They may complain but will still get the work done. They are concerned with their day-to-day job and overall performance. Their main goals are to avoid layoff, continue with their paycheck, and balance home and work life. A majority of the people in the world operate at the middle level. The root of most of the lack of employee engagement and slowdown in our business world and in our lives is due to attachment.

Then come the people who are at the top of the pyramid. These are the people who are **detached**. They worship work, and to them, the work is divine. They aren't attached to failure, success, or any personal outcomes. They work to solve greater problems. They adopt the vision, values, and purpose of the organization they work for. They become passionate contributors, exceed expectations, and stun their colleagues. They are always looking at the company's bigger picture and have a collaborative outlook. They work on a project with full dedication without worrying about success or failure. They are the ones who last the longest in the company and work towards solving pressing issues. They believe only in high-quality work. They consider themselves to be a vital part of the business. They strive to become better today than they were yesterday. These are the self-directed, exceptional leaders. These are the people who achieve unstoppable success, because their productivity is at the peak. Only a small percentage of the people in the organization and world at large are at this level of the pyramid. That is why the gap between exceptional leaders and average leaders is so prominent.

So, let me ask you to take a pause and reflect on this pyramid. Ask yourself, at what level on this pyramid am I? If you are running an organization, where do you see most of your people operating at? In the following pages, I will share with you more about how you can bring more people to become highly detached and fully engaged. You can turn the tables for yourself too.

The Origins of Peace

There is a difference between being attached and being concerned. Attachment means we are afraid and that the element of uncertainty only intensifies our fears. Concern means we are focusing on solutions. The best way to be creative in your work and life, and the best way to succeed with speed is to be detached. Being detached does not mean lack of feeling or emotion. It is not a synonym for indifference, carelessness, or passivity. Acting with detachment means doing the right thing for its own sake, because it needs to be done, without worrying about success or failure. Detachment does not mean that you own nothing. It simply and powerfully means *nothing owns you*. Nothing and no one can disturb your peace of mind. Those operating at the peak of the

FME pyramid are the people who aren't disturbed by results. Results cannot overpower them. They find peace and success within them and operate with a feeling of fulfillment even when challenged.

Let me share with you a story about a king who had a fascination with paintings. One day, he decided to offer a very valuable prize to the artist who would paint a beautiful picture depicting peace. On the judging day, many artists brought their paintings with the hope of winning that valuable prize. The king looked at all the paintings and selected two. The king now had to choose one of the two paintings for the prize. The first painting was a calm lake with clear water. The lake was a perfect mirror to the towering mountains surrounding it. Above it was a blue sky with white fluffy clouds like cotton balls floating in space. It was a perfect masterpiece representing peace. The second painting had mountains too; rugged, dry and bare. Above these mountains was an angry sky overcast with dark clouds, lightning, and a massive downpour of rain. Cascading down one side of the mountain was a ferocious waterfall. No one could initially see peace in this painting. As the king looked closer, though, he saw behind the waterfall the branch of a bush growing out of a crack in the rock. On the branch was a mother bird who had made a nest. And she was very peacefully and affectionately feeding her little ones. Which painting of the two do you think the king choose for his valuable prize? Which painting would you choose? The king chose the second painting. He knew that peace does not necessarily mean being in a place where there is no noise, no hard work, no conflicts, and no trouble. Peace means being in the middle of all the noise and problems and yet remaining calm, staying focused, and moving ahead. Detachment brings us towards this inner peace and focus amidst all our work problems and challenges. That is the real meaning of being detached. It means moving towards your dreams and achieving your goals without anything disturbing you. We have been given our job, business, role, title, money, team, mind, and body to use for a specific purpose. But a slight conflict with a colleague, a little problem with our boss, or the news of a layoff disturbs our mind. Again, a promotion, a bonus, or a new car all changes our state of mind to happiness and excitement. All of this means that circumstances and people own you. And when the mind is a slave of anything, it's attachment. You are on a constant roller coaster ride based on what happens around you. When the mind is not a slave of anything, it is calm and at peace; therefore, it can lead and make clear decisions in any situation. The only difference between people who collapse after failure or loss and those who start again quickly is that the latter know and practice the art of detachment.

One of the hallmarks of effective leadership is this ability to distance oneself from a work situation and to look at it with detachment. I recall one CEO who decided based on industry trends to project a flat growth year. When he presented his analysis for the year to his peers, he was shocked to hear some of them challenge his decision by saying things like, "Why don't you just go relax at the beach if you can't find any alternatives?" The CEO knew he hadn't come up with the best of solutions. Clearly, his mind was worried with thoughts of the past and future results. He decided to seek other alternatives for growing the business. He applied my FME pyramid by first being detached from the worry of the results. And he did indeed grow his business 17% that year; something he couldn't have done without the push to a new level of exploration.

In contrast, Sheila, the CEO of an advertising firm, didn't realize the importance of detachment. In an attempt to meet her sales quota, she focused so heavily on achieving sales results that customer satisfaction was sidelined. Her mind was always stressed, she was angry and constantly worked in fear of not achieving the desired numbers. This slowly began to affect her health, and of course, business was negatively impacted. She remained at the bottom of the FME pyramid. So how do you develop the ability to detach yourself from a situation so that you look at the key factors from a new place? How can you and your people operate at the peak of the pyramid? Among the most effective ways I've observed is the practice of the law of impermanence. But before we can understand this law, let's take a look at the clues that reveal if you work in an attached or detached manner.

Clues You Are Actively or Passively Attached	Clues You Are Detached
Living with increasing levels of fear	Less fear more confidence
Constant feeling of unsatisfied desires	Rising level of expectations from self
Attached to expectations from others	Trusting in others more
Micro-managing everything and everyone	Bouncing back quickly from failures
Slow progress	No ego or greed
Clouded thinking with negativity	Easier to keep your balance
Rise in ego or greed	Accepting both positive and negative events with equanimity
Increase in insecurity and worry	
Things and events begin to own you	Enjoying success and learning from failure
Always under pressure	Remaining calm
Productivity and performance drop	Mood and emotions in control and balanced
Anger rises	Happiness regardless of results
Emotions vary too often	Collaboration focus
Wanting to control everything	Focus on your actions and process
Focus on end result only	Feeling in charge of inner leader

Law of Impermanence

This law has played a critical role in my life and in the lives of millions of people I see succeeding and failing. The one who understands this law and applies it with full faith in their daily life can begin to experience a massive change in self and eventually in outcomes. It eases you through times of transition and pain. You experience the feeling of bliss amidst all the chaos. This is a fact. There is no escape. It is the core of business, one of the most crucial yet most neglected aspects of leadership. The law of impermanence is one of the essential doctrines of Hinduism and Buddhism and is applicable universally. It also appears in Greek philosophy in the writings of *Heraclitus* who is credited with the famous saying, "No man ever steps in the same river twice."

The law of impermanence states that all that exists is temporary; nothing lasts. It emphasizes uncertainty and unpredictability. Therefore, nothing can be grasped or held onto. All relationships and situations will end or change. When we don't fully appreciate this simple but profound truth, we suffer in business and life. So does this mean one

should leave everything, surrender, and go to the Himalaya to meditate? Absolutely not! Do just the opposite. Work harder, *because* you
know nothing is permanent. It *will* pass. As will the good times. As will
the bad times. As will the businesses that you build, and the relationships you develop. As will success and the failure. All of it. All of it at
some point will cease to exist, as you either cease to exist or situations
evolve. And because you know everything is impermanent, you've got
to work harder every day. This mindset now makes you unstoppable.
Let's explore some real-life examples that will help us understand the
importance and depth of this law.

Life Is Like a Stock Market

I met Vinod at one of my client's annual dinner events. In our conversation, I got to know more of Vinod, a director in my client's firm.
Vinod had been the co-founder of a huge investment management
firm. When his firm was as its peak, Vinod's lifestyle was envied by
many. Seven luxury cars, a 16,026 square-foot house with a private
beach, around-the-world travel in his private jet, and of course, the
billion-dollar bank balance. He had it all. He was often quoted in
interviews about how great life was. His investment funds invested
heavily in internet and technology companies. Then, the market
crashed badly in 2000. Returns from his funds fell in tandem, due to
which Vinod could not keep up his pledges to various stakeholders.
He suffered heavy losses. His property was seized as he was unable to
pay the loans. He lost all his money and possessions to repay debts. He
was forced to apply for a job, and as luck would have it, he got a job
at the same office where he had started off eighteen years before. As he
stepped into the office, he said to himself, "Everything in life is impermanent. At one point I was at the top, and today I am down. Life is
like a stock market, it will take me up again someday." Listening to
him today, I was reminded of a quote by Isaac Newton, "What goes
up must come down."

Things Can Change at Any Moment, Suddenly

In another instance, I interacted with a surgeon in Denver. I was talking to him about the law of impermanence and how practicing it affects our lives positively. The surgeon added that even from a scientific point of view, the law of impermanence is true. Cell divisions take place in each living being continuously. Old cells in our bodies die and are replaced continuously with new ones. Every moment, many thoughts arise and die in each individual. Psychologically and physically one is never the same all the time. Technically speaking, no individual is ever composed of the same amount of energy and cellular material all the time. He is subject to change and change is in continuous movement. The surgeon then gave me a classic example from one of his patients. He said this man was brought to the hospital in a vegetative state due to a sudden brain injury. After examining his condition and administering initial treatment, he was sent to the rehabilitation center. Every day, this man's son, an executive director of a huge firm, would come to meet his father at intervals of three hours. He would talk and behave with him as if everything were normal, as if his father could listen and comprehend everything that the son said. Whenever this doctor visited the patient and saw the son talk so passionately and "normally," with the hope that his father would respond, he would intervene saying, "Young man, nothing will change, your dad has gone into a vegetative state, and it's been eight years now. Medical science reports and all top surgeons who have examined your father have said that he will never recover and now has only two years to live." But the son would not give up on his father and continued the same routine each day. He moved him every day at intervals of three hours, for eight years to keep him from getting bedsores. One day, to everyone's amazement, this man awoke from his vegetative state by showing that he could move his fingers. Today, he is still in the rehab and has recovered 75% of his former function.

The doctor smiled and said to me, "Yes, nothing is permanent. Things can change at any moment, suddenly." I concluded that though

science has its own reasons for the man's recovery, the law of impermanence was definitely visible here and can be seen in every situation.

No One Knows What Tomorrow Will Bring

Victoria, a marketing undergraduate with just a C grade in her class,
became a salesgirl with a mid-sized computer assembly and service company. She was honest and hardworking. The company's culture was such
that in an aim to secure more client contracts in the market, it began to
acquire large client contracts through bribery. In such a corrupt company culture, Victoria's honesty brought her demotion and humiliation.
People condemned her for her work ethic in the industry and said, "you
will never get anywhere in life." Some commented, "You will always
remain a loser," while others showed off their high commissions and promotions to her saying, "She will remain where she is." Somehow, Victoria
continued with her work. She had a passion for serving customers. This
passion made her realize that sales success is dependent on the customer;
so if the customer is satisfied and happy with the service, then bribery
will not be necessary to secure these contracts. She tried to explain this
philosophy to her colleagues and boss, but no one agreed with her.

Victoria remained firm in her belief, resigned from the company
and started her own. Her strategic goal continued to be customer service and customer satisfaction as opposed to just selling the product
through bribes and providing zero customer service. With her hard
work and honesty still intact, the company soon became successful
because of its dedication to excellent customer service. Although it did
not make much profit, she was able to hire a small team of three people
and continued to make a huge difference. Soon she became a threat to
her previous company, whose sales started to decrease as many clients
canceled their orders and placed orders at Victoria's company. Victoria's
company rose to great success and one morning a leading newspaper
carried an interview with her. She had become a great success! Those
who once condemned her now praised her work ethic and wanted to
join her firm.

No one knows what tomorrow will bring. Think of all the stories we hear of people going from rags to riches and riches to rags. Things change, people change, and times change. When you feel like utter garbage, know that it won't last. When you are sitting on top of the world, that too will end. Humans tend to forget that no condition is permanent. One who has the ability to accept this truth will remain stable in the face of failure and success, sadness and happiness. Everything changes and those who learn to detach are the leaders who can outlast the competition in the game called business.

The law of impermanence calls us to do the very best we can and leave the rest. Move on as if you've already received it. Change and separation is woven in the fabric of our lives. This is the basic law of nature. Mother Nature herself operates in duality. There is day and night, life and death, active and inactive, heat and cold, cause and effect. It is rightly said, "Yet you do not know what tomorrow will bring. What is your life? For you are a mist that appears for a little time and then vanishes" (James 4:13).

As leaders, we are taught about change, we speak about change, and yet we want to avoid change. We get disturbed in our career life not because things are impermanent but because we believe things are *permanent*. This illusion of remaining in a state of permanence is what causes many leaders to slow down. It is the primary cause of stress in the workplace. When you develop the power to detach, you achieve absolute freedom from the problem of attachment. When you realize that everything in the business sphere is impermanent, you accept with your heart that everything in it will come to an end, that is the time you are able to face the ever-changing and disruptive professional world fearlessly and afresh.

Have you ever seen a tree laden with fruit? Its branches are bent, as if it's surrendering its fruits to you. The tree understands that only when it surrenders will it be able to produce new fruit (and ultimately, more trees like itself). Similarly, when you surrender, you will accelerate your influence and effectiveness as a leader. A leader who surrenders has conquered his mind and optimized the inner leader within. His work is divine, and he finds joy in the process, not the result. He is able to steadily move from one goal to another and achieve true success from within. He does achieve whatever he dreams of. An awareness of uncertainty, of impermanence, is a powerful motivator for us to make the most of the here and now. Let nothing own you, while you still own everything. Let me give you a golden mantra that will enable you to be focused and succeed each day at whatever you do.

Mantra: "I will give my best each day and leave the rest."

MANTRA 5

Transform Pain to Purpose

Pain—a feeling that almost everyone wants to avoid, whether emotional or physical. My father would often say, "No living entity in this world, be it human or animal, is free from pain. Pain is inevitable, but suffering is your choice." How true. Much of the suffering we identify with and experience through our pain is entirely within our heads. It comes from the stories we build up around the pain and that we become consumed by. Much of our suffering is in our attempts to resist pain. When your boss insults you or speaks rudely to you, any suffering you continue to feel after the words have been spoken will be playing entirely within your mind. It's your emotional response to the pain that makes you suffer, not the pain itself.

Stories of Working Through Pain

The year 2015 was crucial for Tanya, who worked at one of the premier luxury magazines in London. This was the year when the current editor was resigning and must choose his successor. Tanya had been aiming for this position and had worked tirelessly towards it. She was smart and talented, and was certain she deserved this position. She had a great relationship with the editor as well as those in his inner circle. On June 25, 2015, the editor announced Harry as the new editor. Tanya was upset at being passed over for promotion and began feeling disheartened and frustrated. She started telling herself, "What were they thinking? What's the point of all my efforts if they're just going to pass right over me? After all I've sacrificed, this is what I get! This is the third time they have done this to me." She began developing a feeling of hatred towards the new editor and would often be found at the office in a sulky mood. Anyone who spoke to her would hear her repeat the unfair promotion incident and sulk over it. She struggled to deal with her emotions. It's been three years since that incident now, and though she has moved jobs, Tanya still feels depressed and experiences the pain. A once normally cheerful and happy to chat with everyone at work person, today just can't bring herself out of this slump. She's finding it so hard to recover.

While for some of us reading this real-life incident may mean little, for many who nurture dreams of growth, promotion, and success, this comes as a big blow to their professional life. And the pain isn't always about being passed over for promotion.

Marshall experienced a tremendous pain when he was constantly losing his clients to competitors despite all the work and talent. Eventually, after eight years, he had to shut down his business. The pain of feeling like a loser persisted. And it happened with Sangeeta who faced racism at work despite being a great Java developer. And then what about Irene, a genealogist who had to leave her well-established practice in London to move to Beijing, China, where her husband was offered a lucrative position? The pain of loneliness and feeling unfulfilled took her into depression.

When I sat with Tanya for her one-to-one coaching, when I spoke with Marshall at an event I was invited to speak at, when I got to know Irene on a plane, and when I had coffee with Sangeeta, I realized that most of our pains are self-inflicted. And every day we bring this pain to our work. You must have gauged from these incidents that I am talking here about the emotional pain that we experience at our workplaces or because of our work. Emotional pain is of a non-physical origin and generates an unpleasant feeling. A pioneer in the field of suicidology, Edwin S. Shneidman, described it as, "How much you hurt as a human being." Emotional pain happens when you didn't expect a certain action or reaction from others, you get an unexpected response, and you feel hurt. It begins to disturb your inner leader.

Emotional Iceberg Principle

Emotional pain is often buried deep within, and its consequences are seen in your actions and results; just like an iceberg where only a small fraction is visible above the water line, with most of the ice hiding below the surface. Most of our pain and suffering stays beneath the surface too. Every one of us can see the outcomes of suffering, though, like lack of productivity, unresolved workplace conflicts, gossip, broken communication, micromanagement, mistrust, professional grudges, and other negative behaviors. Figure 5.1 illustrates what I call the emotional iceberg principle.

Look around you at your workplace. Do you see unresolved interpersonal conflicts, broken communication, stress, mistrust, micromanagement, gossip, harassment, and low motivation? The reason is deep

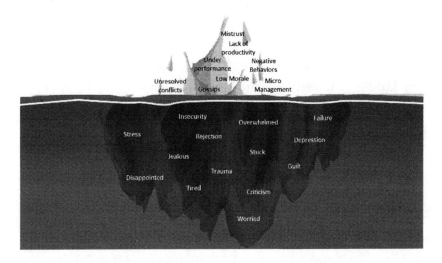

Figure 5.1 *The Emotional Iceberg Principle.*

rooted and lies in the emotional pain that people endure and carry to their workplace. Of course, no one talks about this since the workplace is seen as an environment where employees are meant to maintain a facade of hard-working, focused perfection. We work in a culture that makes accommodations for physical pain but expects us to deal with emotional pain on our own time, while continuing to get up, drive to work, achieve deadlines and goals, complete assignments, motivate teams, and act like we lead a fulfilling work life.

In fact, when you feel emotional pain, the same areas of the brain get activated as when you feel physical pain: the anterior insula and the anterior cingulate cortex. The science of epigenetics demonstrates that emotional pain affects us at the cellular level, turning on and off the genes related to our immune system. Neuroscience has proven that the human mind is wired to avoid pain and seek happiness. The mind always gravitates towards happiness, pleasure, and success. But because we do not know how to shift from pain to happiness, we either ignore the pain, learn to live with it, or deal with it in negative ways. And because the subject is considered taboo, how do you think people are dealing with it? To cope with this inner unease, people have resorted to various means of pain disposal such as

- Denial
- Withdrawal
- Acquiring power
- Indulging in every imaginable distraction to divert the mind
- Demanding attention from loved ones
- Reacting impulsively
- Bullying
- Self-harm
- Over-working
- Mind-altering substance use.

We have two choices when we experience pain: one is to pay attention to it and take the necessary corrective actions, and the other is to ignore in any or all of the ways just listed until the engine overheats and is no longer capable of taking us to our destination. Our emotional engine is telling us to pull over as soon as possible, investigate the root cause of the emotional pain, make necessary repairs, and then change driving habits. But we're often not addressing the real driver of our pain. In the following pages, I am going to share with you precise methods of taking the leap from emotional pain to emotional stability that are fundamental to achieving unstoppable success.

The Neuroscience of Emotional Pain

I had an opportunity to sit across the table and talk with Dr. Senthil Radhakrishnan, the Administrative Chief and Clinical Neurosurgical PA from the Department of Neurosurgery at Duke Hospital and a Guest Lecturer at the Duke PA Program. I asked him what happens to the brain when emotional pain builds up. He said emotional pain, if prolonged for more than three months, can manifest itself as chronic physical pain and can lead to depression. Emotional pain can mimic the effects of chronic pain and depression and cause structural changes in the brain, especially the areas responsible for memory, mood, and executive functions. This stress can interrupt neurotransmitters in the hippocampus and prevent formation of new neurons, thereby causing a shrinking of the hippocampus. Lack of new neurons impedes memory, learning, and dealing with those emotions, thus creating a vicious cycle. Brain MRIs of people dealing with chronic pain when compared to healthy individuals reveal a smaller hippocampus. The dentate gyrus of the hippocampus is crucial for learning and memory. On the other hand, the amygdala, the tight cluster of nuclei located deep in the brain on either side of the medial temporal lobe, is part of the limbic system and plays a vital role in processing emotion and memory—especially memories associated with fear, anxiety, and motivation. Persistent emotional pain causes hyperactivity in the amygdala and even hypertrophy of the amygdala. Hypertrophied amygdala can cause anxiety disorders and sleep disturbances. Finally, the prefrontal cortex, which is responsible for several functions including regulating emotions and decision making, may atrophy with persistent emotional pain and depression.

I found this interesting. The very elements that shape a leader and are imperative for one's success—good memory, better education, good sleep, and dealing with emotions are impeded because of holding on to emotional pain. When you operate each day at work not knowing how to deal with and heal your emotional pain, you reduce your productivity and creativity. It weighs you down and soon begins to interfere with your progress and success. The consequence of emotional pain can compromise your effectiveness and credibility. You can exercise poor judgment, and it can make you ineffective, unhappy, cost you a promotion, or possibly even your job or business. Dr. Senthil further added that not being able to deal in a timely manner with emotional pain affects us in our work every day; it perpetuates anxiety, depression, and isolation, thus creating ideal conditions for drug and alcohol abuse. Decreased memory and poor sleep often cause fatigue, poor job performance, and disability. Emotional pain's social dysfunction can be seen in one's social life and activities of daily living—job, work at home, parenting skills, sexual function, interpersonal relationships. It also promotes other chronic pain conditions like fibromyalgia, cluster headaches, migraines, irritable bowel syndrome, pelvic pain, etc. Often, it leads to a feeling of helplessness not just from perceived pain but also anticipated pain.

Leading from Pain to Leading from Joy

After hearing Dr. Senthil's views on how prolonged emotional pain affects our brain and our work, I discovered how deeply it affects the organization and its culture. His words reminded me of James, the top senior manager at a sales and marketing company. He had joined the company recently and had grabbed the reins, rebuffing everyone else's advice and efforts. People were working eighteen hours a day in order to meet his deadlines and survive being fired. Snow or storm, he expected people to be there. His management style began to damage the team's confidence. People's productivity dropped. Unfortunately, James refused to see the problems coming. When I was called in to coach James, I sensed his mind was so crammed with old boxes of family-related emotional pain that his ability to experience the here and the now was severely limited. He kept repeating a sentence that had become almost like a spiritual mantra: "My father mistreated me." He told how he was treated badly from the age of seven by a very authoritarian father and was constantly ordered to do things regardless of his desire to do so. I pointed out to James that he had returned to the story of his father mistreating him for at least fifteen times in a span of our one-hour conversation. This is a pain story he tells himself many a times in the course of the day. This pain did not allow him to sleep well most nights and left him operating all day with a feeling of anxiety. He preferred isolation and would often complain of constant headaches— he blamed work pressure for all of this. His negative behavior at work could definitely be attributed to his emotional pain. It kept him from engaging in a healthy work relationship with his people. He believed in an authoritarian way of leading because that's all he'd ever known. When I now think about James, I realize there were structural changes in his brain because of his experience. Look around you. Are you or any of your people behaving negatively at work? The cause is deeper.

It's no surprise that emotional pain from our past can stick to us like super glue. The pain, the suffering become our identity. For some people, a tragic event that happened in the recent or even the distant past still brings great sorrow. Radhika, an entrepreneur and a good friend of mine, is an example of how we allow our minds to dwell on negative experiences when we should have let them go long ago moved on with our lives. Radhika constantly reminds herself and speaks about her boss who happened to sexually harass her by sending her suggestive emails and handwritten letters. This went on for a period of time, and it affected Radhika's personal and professional life. After a long time, she mustered the courage to complain about this to the human resources department, and appropriate action was later taken against the boss. This incident happened in her mid-career life. It's been twelve years now since Radhika left that job and got into entrepreneurship. However, she keeps reminding herself of the experience and speaks about it to whomever she can. Not only is this affecting her personally, her business too is facing the consequences because she often doubts people. Most of us lead from pain. Dwelling on the possible causes of emotional pain is more likely to exacerbate than ameliorate it. I would encourage you to reflect upon some questions. Do you ever feel you are paying too much attention to your emotional pain? Do you or your people easily accumulate emotional pain? Now, you may be saying, "But Payal, it's impossible to keep track of emotional pain and bandage it." True. People today are flooded with meetings, emails, deadlines, travel, and presentations. We are in an age of speed. Where is the time to speak about anyone's pain? In the rush and pressure of our work days, our minds are preoccupied by the stream of thoughts. Most of us think our feelings of emotional pain are irrelevant and messy to deal with. But you, your team, and your organization cannot go far when you lead from pain. Sooner or later performance will drop. And then all of your workplace problems step up to get your attention. If you observe closely, you will notice that emotional pain changes your state of mind. For many people, outside circumstances and other people's behaviors dictate their state of mind. When things go their way—they get that promotion or buy the big house—everything looks set, and their pain subsides. And when things do not go their way—they get fired, face losses, and get transferred to another department, and the new boss is horrible—things look messy, and their pain returns and is magnified. They enter into a state of victimhood. Most people continue on this seesaw ride of emotional pain. Those who are exceptional leaders are very conscious of one important equation:

Emotional pain = State of mind

They do not allow any emotional pain to affect their state of mind. They are constantly working to maintain a healthy state of mind. They lead from joy. I call it an *empowered leader state of mind*. Everyone must move from a paralyzed leader state of mind (negativity and disbelief) to an empowered leader state of mind (being in charge). Once you begin to take care of your state of mind, you automatically deal with emotional pain in a positive way. You begin to lead with joy. As John Burroughs rightly puts it, "The kingdom of heaven is not a place but a state of mind." It is an inside job. Blaming your boss, the environment, and other people only means that you will continue to suffer. And suffering is a choice. Emotional pain when left unattended leads to a negative work atmosphere. This is why, for a healthy work culture, for your success, both personally and professionally, and for your good health and progress, you must take the responsibility to not just deal but heal your emotional pain.

The rules for work are changing. We are being judged by a new yardstick—how well we handle ourselves and each other. This new yardstick predicts who will be an achiever, who will move ahead, and who will be known as a peak performer. I once was invited to speak with army cadets. I learned from them that apart from leading a disciplined life and the rigorous physical training, they are taught how to make friends with discomfort, how to triumph over adversity, and how to bounce back quickly from failures. In your work life, tragic events such as layoffs, being passed over for promotions, death, forceful retirement, bad team relationships, failing business, work overload, lack of rewards, and demotions are inevitable. A friend of mine at a Fortune 500 company told me how terrible he feels when the company downsizes, and he has to demote, transfer, or let go of people. "There is no work guarantee these days," he constantly reminds me. The sense that despite all the hard and long hours, you will no longer retire with a gold watch creeps in. As the Buddha taught, we are each given ten thousand joys and ten thousand sorrows. The sooner one manages to summon up enough courage to overcome pain in order not to be deprived of the opportunity to lead a normal and happy life, the better it will surely be.

And it's possible. Dr. Senthil affirms that structural changes caused in the brain due to prolonged emotional pain can be reversed. He puts emphasis on exercise as a healer since the endorphins released during exercise help relieve pain. He further adds that one must seek help, consider biofeedback, meditate, and do yoga.

The Giant Leap—from Victim to Unstoppable Leader

If you want better results and to achieve unstoppable success, you've got to take the leap from being a victim to being an unstoppable leader. And this leap happens when you move out of emotional pain and enter into emotional stability. Emotional stability is a zone where you are balanced, your thoughts are calm, and they are aligned with your inner self. It's a zone of fulfillment, happiness, and success. While in this zone, regardless of the circumstances, you are able to make great decisions. Emotional stability is a culture every organization and entrepreneur must strive to achieve. To get into the stability zone, the first step is to follow what I call the "Power of Five." The Power of Five says that once you experience emotional pain, give yourself five minutes to cry, feel the self-sabotage, and go through the experience. These five minutes are yours to feel the feelings. After five minutes, it's time to change your state to an empowered one. Almost all of my clients have benefited tremendously from the Power of Five. It has helped them to quickly get into action and resist the urge to stay upset or give up on themselves. Once you have practiced the Power of Five, the following 3R's will help you take the leap into the stability zone:

1. **Release:** During my sessions, I often tell a joke to the audience, and they burst into laughter. I then repeat the joke and some from the audience laugh again. I repeat the joke for the third time, but no one laughs. I am sure you are thinking, "Who would laugh at the same joke again and again?" Well, this is exactly what I tell

my audience. When you cannot laugh at the same joke again, why do you talk about and cry over the same pain again and again? Releasing pain is a pure vibration of feeling from within. Begin by exploring within; what is it that leads to so much turmoil in you and is not letting you get off the worry and hurt? When you search within deeply, there is a positive change in your system, and you become more empathetic. Remind yourself of the one who has caused this hurt—perhaps they were also in pain. Whatever they did, they did within the limitations of their understanding at that time. This thought helps release the pain within and will make you feel light. And only a light kite can fly high. Recognize the emotions you go through when in pain and choose to release the body sensations that are triggered with that emotion. When an issue is resolved through the process of releasing, the memory of the emotional incident remains but the negative charge associated with it disappears. The results are unbelievably fast and most of the time permanent. We have limited space inside of us, and if you are holding pain inside yourself, you cannot give space to creativity, innovation, and happiness. If you're someone who wants to live a deeply fulfilling work life, then you must practice the art of releasing the pain. Letting go is one of the most courageous acts of leadership.

2. **Reframe:** Have you ever thought what the root cause of your emotional pain is? It has been said that we are meaning-make machines. Most of our pain comes from the meaning we give to the event, not from the event or experience itself. Reframing is the ability to look at a situation in a new way, giving it a more insightful meaning. Shakespeare said it best: "There is nothing either good or bad but thinking makes it so." If someone at work ignores you, do you immediately assume that they have something against you? They are busy? Maybe they hate you? Or they simply missed seeing you? Whatever meaning you decide to give to the event, how you reframe your thinking around it will decide how you will feel as well as what your next action will be.

The meaning each person attaches to the same event is crucial. Events are powerless. They are meaningless. They keep changing. It is you who gives them life and power by the meaning you associate with that event or person. We see everything through our own filters and beliefs. It's all about the color of your glasses. What color are your glasses? Most events in life are neutral. Do you see the best in people and situations? Do you actively look for the best? You are going to give a meaning to things anyway. So why not give it the best meaning? Think about how else you can look at it. The pain you are going through is independent of people and situations. It is only dependent on your thoughts. It has been proven that people behave and respond very differently under similar circumstances because of differences in the meaning they assign to that circumstance; one may make himself miserable, while the other may still remain joyous. Many successful people have given the meaning of "opportunity" to failures and adversity. There are two categories of people. One who makes the situation smaller by reframing it positively. The other who make the same situation bigger than what it is by reframing it with a negative perception. Next time something doesn't go as planned, change how you see things. And if you aren't able to give a positive meaning to whatever happens in your life, then don't make the effort to give it a negative one either. Mark Batterson captured this idea well when he said, "It's not our experiences that make us or break us. It's our interpretation of and explanation for those experiences that ultimately determines who we become. Your explanations are more important than your experiences" (*Soulprint*, 62–63).

3. **Regain:** This is a process where you regain control over your inner leader. The more self-confident you are, the more likely you will succeed at this step. You can regain control over your inner leader once you acknowledge what your current situation might have to teach you. Resolve to change. Follow any real positive growth with action. You have to *do* things differently. This is

where your pain can truly turn into your greatest power. You can do many things to regain control over your inner leader: meditate, express gratitude, read self-help books for positive inspiration, or enroll in a course.

What's difficult about leadership is that nobody ever sits you down and "teaches" you what being a real leader is all about. Whenever I think about the topic of leadership, I feel incredibly blessed to have had the mentors I did. At the time, I didn't understand how much I was learning by just being around them and listening to them on a daily basis. But as I navigated through my own work life and later started my own company, I realized the massive impact they had had on my development. At the age of twenty-three, I was sitting across the table from the CEO of a large organization discussing growth strategies. I realized how important it was for them to be calm when everyone else is stressed. This is why it's important that as a leader you know how to manage your emotional pain and how to heal any emotional pain. You can't afford to carry this emotional baggage and expect to deliver great results.

The reason it's important to heal your pain is because your cells are incredibly clever little units. They remember everything—every pain, every thought, every message. And as the old cells die, they transfer their memories to future generations of cells. This memory allows the cells to "retain a record of past emotional pains to sharpen their responses next time." Over the last fifty years, experts have verified that the source of our symptoms of pain and anxiety is usually not located in our body generally or even in our environment. The source is located in what science calls "cellular memory." So when you constantly engage in self-sabotage based on your emotional pain, your thoughts get stuck in cellular memory. When you operate daily in a state of pain and hurt, you create poor quality thoughts that prevent you from using your full potential and achieving great results. Quantum physics says that every thought or emotion has its own vibrational frequency or wave frequency. So, when you operate at a low frequency, you attract everything that exists at that frequency level. This is why when you continue to hold onto emotional pain of any kind, you experience similar incidents despite changing your job, country, and boss. It can pull you back into the emotional pain zone. When you change your thinking and raise its frequency level, you change your experience of the situation. This single factor has the potential to dramatically alter the course of your results. You can choose to view a situation in such a way that validates your reasons for feeling stressed, or you can view it so that you feel motivated and up for the challenge to deal with it. I believe we are all capable of creating new neural pathways in our brains that allow us to manage our emotional pain. One of the most powerful paths to emotional healing I have observed is to transform your pain into a deeply rooted purpose. This is when the healing process can unfold naturally, and when it does, you will experience relief and a surge of well-being. You begin to see better results in your life, and your organization creates more space for creativity and innovation.

The Transformation—from Seed of Pain to Seed of Purpose

There was this museum laid with beautiful marble tiles, with a huge marble statue displayed in the middle of the lobby. Many people came from all over the world just to admire this beautiful marble statue.

One night, the marble tiles started talking to the marble statue.

Marble tile: "Marble statue, it's just not fair, it's just not fair! Why does everybody from all over the world come all the way here just to step on me while admiring you? Not fair!"

Marble statue: "My dear friend, marble tile. Do you still remember that we were actually from the same cave?"

Marble tile: "Yeah! That's why I feel it is even more unfair. We were born from the same cave and yet we receive different treatment now. Not fair!"

Marble statue: "Do you still remember the day when the designer tried to work on you, but you resisted the tools?"

Marble tile: "Yes, of course I remember. I hate that guy! How could he use those tools on me! It hurt so badly!"

Marble statue: "That's right! He couldn't work on you at all as you resisted being worked on."

Marble tile: "So???"

Marble statue: "When he decided to give up on you and start working on me instead, I knew at once that I would be something different after his efforts. I did not resist his tools, instead I bore all the painful tools he used on me."

Marble tile: "Hmmmmm …."

Marble statue: "My friend, there is a price to everything in life. Since you decided to give up halfway, you can't blame anybody who steps on you now."

To succeed and to be the best, you've got to be like the marble statue. The harder the knocks you go through in life, the more you learn and put them to use in the future. Rather than feeling like a victim, think of the end result and be a leader. Every pain has a reason, a deeply rooted reason. Your job is to shift your focus from the pain to the purpose. All great business ideas that have succeeded are because their leaders saw an existing pain in the world and wanted to heal it. Similarly, with the emotional pain clearly identified, switch gears and develop cures. I urge you to take a pause here, deep breathe and reflect on the following: What is your great purpose? What clear unmistakable message is coming from inside of you? It's telling you about the purpose you should be living for. You have to determine what to do *in* your pain, and what to do *with* your pain. Take Candy Lightner as an example. She founded one of the country's largest activist organizations, Mothers Against Drunk Driving, after her daughter died in a drunk driving accident. What is your story? Are you building up all the emotional pain inside of you or are you using it constructively? Are you transforming your pain to a purpose?

The most successful people I know of are leaders who know how to harness their emotional pain as a way to bring out the best in themselves and in others. One of the ways to transform your emotional pain to a deeply rooted purpose is to check your PAQ. PAQ stands for either pain-associated questions or purpose-associated questions.

Pain-Associated Question	Purpose-Associated Questions
Why did this have to happen to me?	How can I use this?
Why is life unfair to me?	Why is this important to me?
What did I do to deserve this?	What positive outcome will this bring?
Who is to blame?	What is working in this situation?
Why am I such a loser?	What three changes must I make to improve my life?
What's the problem with me?	How do I navigate my way ahead?
When will I be out of this?	How can I minimize the possibility of this happening again?

Observe how our mind makes things worse for us when we ask ourselves pain-associated questions? It elicits a negative answer that will undoubtedly inspire negative thinking, and you know where that leads. Similarly, the answers we get when we ask ourselves purpose-associated questions help us to completely change our perspective and life. I always say that our mind is like a search engine. The type of answer you get is determined by the type of questions you ask. Martin Luther King, Jr. famously said, "There is a power in the universe that is able to make a way out of no way." The universe answers every question that we ask, but the problem is that most people ask disempowering pain-associated questions.

Becoming Iconic

In my work with champions and leaders, I have identified five zones one must pass through to break through emotional pain and achieve success. Each zone has its own learning. I've already spoken to you about each zone. Greatness begins beyond your pain zone. As you

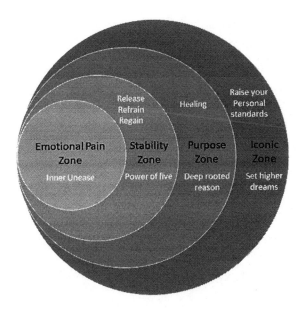

Figure 5.2   *The Transformation.*

begin to move outside of the pain zone, you begin to set higher goals and raise personal standards. Figure 5.2 explains in a nutshell the journey from emotional pain to success. Every individual can break through.

In every person's life, there comes a time of ultimate challenge. A time when things seem unfair. A time when your faith and values are tested beyond limits. Use these tests as opportunities to become a better person. Don't allow these experiences to destroy you. Don't let it create a flood of emotional pain. Do not be discouraged by setbacks and failures. In every emotional pain you experience, begin to release, reframe, and regain. The universe works in ways that are unknown to humans. The universe is brewing up a greater purpose that will outlast your pain, but it needs your support. Regardless of the source of the pain, begin to use your pain to accomplish a greater purpose. Don't waste your pain. Instead, redeem it. And as you begin to heal your pain by now shifting your focus to your deeply rooted purpose, you shape a new character and personality for yourself. You will discover a new natural high. All of this will bring about a massive change in your actions, as a result of which you can build your own true success. When you take the leap, you will be able to grow in ways that you never have before. Are you going to embrace your pain and reinvent, or are you just going to wallow? You have to make a choice!

Mantra: "I am not controlled by my pain."

MANTRA 6

Elevate the Self

Before you read further, I want you to experiment with something. I want you to imagine that you are holding a container in your hand. Now imagine you are taking this container and walking towards a huge ocean filled with clear blue water so you can fill your container. Take a pause and check the size of your container. Is it extra small, small, medium, large, or extra large? Reflect on this—did I ever mention what the size the container must be? No. Then, what made you limit your container size? Why wasn't it limitless or as big as you could imagine it to be? Or maybe it was. The size of the container you chose represents many areas of your work life. It tells you what you think about yourself. It sends subtle signals to people about what they should think about you, and it tells you what the size of your goal or dream is. The huge ocean with clear blue water represents opportunities and failures. The size of your container shows your capacity to accept these opportunities and failures. I have people who come to me during workshop break time and tell me that their bosses do not see their value and that they underpay them. I tell them that your boss sees your value to be just as much as you believe your value to be. You are worth as much as you think you are. You will get as much as you think you deserve.

Leaders make sure that their people see the organization's vision, but if your vision about yourself and your business dream isn't limitless, your team and organization will fail to trust not only the vision but most importantly you as a leader. Too many of us are afraid to think big.

So, we give up on our dreams and follow the crowd. We remain average though our skills are exceptional. We dream of becoming the CEO of the company, but limit our thinking to a manager level. We want to expand our business and build an empire, but think only of ways to survive in the business. We want to create an impact on the world, but think mostly of how to keep our job and have the paycheck coming. In fact, I have met numerous people globally who have stopped imagining they could be anything great in their work life. This thinking of theirs not only limits their own progress but also hinders the growth of the organization. The quality of the majority of your people's thinking determines how far your organization will go. And the quality of your thinking will define the level of your success. Nothing will go beyond your thinking. Your actions will be limited by your thinking. During one of my coaching sessions with an artist—a good man who had achieved a modest success—he told me he felt he had already reached his limits in life. One day, I attended a painting exhibition with him where he stopped to admire one of the paintings by Vincent Van Gogh. As he gazed at this beautiful and famous art piece, he commented to me, "I can't even imagine being like Vincent Van Gogh and having my painting exhibited at a place like this." I looked at him and said with a smile, "Don't worry. You won't. Your paintings will never reach the heights of success that Van Gogh's did."

Startled, he looked at me and said in a slightly irritated voice, "What do you mean not going to happen for me?"

In a relaxed tone I replied, "As long as you can't imagine it, then it's not going to happen for you." There was silence between us. He realized how his own thinking was condemning him to mediocrity.

People say it takes courage to do something big in life. I say it takes courage to *think* something big. Many of us have assumed that we've already peaked in our work life. That we will never be any more successful. And sadly, we will be proved right if we continue to think that way. When you say to yourself that you can't go any further, your actions will follow your expectations. Only when you think big, only when you expand the size of your container, can you do something big.

The size of the container is your attitude, your confidence, your thoughts, and your energy. It is that currency with which people transact—psychological currency—so begin to increase its value.

Boiled down to its true essence, it is all about elevating the self. If you do not elevate the self from within, you will always remain average. Why do you think companies aren't seeing a drive in their people despite all the training? Why is innovation not at its peak in all organizations? Why is it that people come up with great ideas, but the execution is weak? This is because most companies are paying so much attention to numbers that they forget it's the people who ultimately deliver the results. It's the people who execute strategies and make important decisions. I have been helping people and companies execute strategies to increase their market share. What I have noticed is this; most people believe that they have reached their limit in their job and business. So they aren't really inspired to achieve. Because we aren't thinking big, we aren't achieving big. We go to work each day with a limited mentality. Most of us allow our circumstances to determine where we will go in life. For extraordinary achievements, develop an extraordinary level of thinking.

I learned the importance of elevating the self in an interesting way. In 2000, my husband Ashish and I relocated to America for his work assignment. As we settled into a new culture, I began the process of applying for jobs, and in a couple of years, I got an opportunity to work for a mid-size advertising company. I loved my work, the salary, and the people. However, I encountered one problem, a big one for me. My boss and I weren't able to get along. Now don't get me wrong here. She was excellent when it came to the technical aspects of advertising. But when it came to people management, she was not a boss that you would want to work with. Unappreciative, unaware of the team's needs, micromanaging, and unrealistic work expectations became a constant source of friction between the two of us. After eleven months of bearing this, I decided to do what most of us would have done. I submitted my resignation letter. I was confident that I would be able to secure another job within my thirty-day notice period. However, to my surprise the company declined my resignation letter. The vice president of the company met with me and said, "Payal, our CEO is well aware of your work and capabilities. He would like you to continue in another department in an independent role." Did I take that offer? Yes, of course I did. Look, the only problem I had was with my boss. I loved my job and everything else that came with it. So here I was in a new role, new department, new people, and new projects. I worked hard and smart and within a year got promoted to a leadership position. I still remember that December of 2005. The CEO of the company had a ritual of meeting one-to-one for five minutes with the leadership team. It was my first time, and I was excited as I wanted to thank him for what he had done for me. So when it was my turn, as I sat across the table from him, my face gleaming, I said to him, "I want to take this opportunity to thank you for helping me move ahead in my career." He looked at me saying, "I haven't helped you to move ahead. You've in fact gotten yourself stuck and will always be dependent on others for your professional success." Trust me, I was shocked beyond words hearing him say this. And what followed is something that gives me goose bumps even today when I share this incident with my audience and readers. It forever changed the way I think. This sixty-five-year-old CEO looked straight into my eyes and said to me in a deep voice,

Payal, undeniably each of us will in our professional life face challenges, favoritism, frictions, bad relations, deadline pressures, problems, politics, and much more. Each of us will have our share of success and failure. And we all will also be given four options in our professional lives:

Option # 1: Be quiet, keep doing your work and ignore what's happening around you.

Option # 2: Quit and decide to find another job or boss.

Option # 3: Stick around, work with that difficult person but always remain stressed from within and drag yourself to work each day.

Option # 4: Make yourself powerful and elevate yourself to deal with anything.

Everything depends on the option you choose.

Saying this, he looked at his watch, and it was exactly five minutes into our meeting. He got up from the chair and thanked me for my time and left. And I stood there speechless and motionless. At that time, being in my mid-twenties, I did not quite grasp the depth of what he was telling me. But as I navigated through my own career life, with all its ups and downs, I began to truly understand each of his options. I eventually realized that it's best to practice option number four if you want to not just survive but thrive in the corporate world.

Elevate yourself to deal with anything. Let's say, for instance, that you have a problem with your boss or team at your workplace. And let's say you just can't pull it anymore and you decide to resign. So here you are now in a new company, new job, new boss, new opportunities, new salary, new team, and new challenges. But guess what? It's the same old you with the same old patterns of dealing with situations and people. It will take only a slight problem, and you will again be hopping to a new company. Soon enough your career life will be over. You will look back and see how you started off with passion and with the aim of making a difference in the lives of people. But all you ended up doing was hopping from one job to another in search of that perfect team, boss, project, and opportunity. If only you had stayed where you were and finished strong. Because when you finish strong, you give a powerful message to the self that success is within and that you carry it wherever you go. How you deal with people and situations today is what you will carry forward to the next job, the next client, and the next project. What is the guarantee that if you are unhappy in your today that you will be happy in your tomorrow? What is the guarantee that if tomorrow you move on to a new company and have a great boss, that boss will never be replaced with one that's hard to get along with? If you want to progress and succeed, then know that all your problems and challenges today are the fertile ground that are helping you to grow. Have you ever seen an object whose temperature was raised on its own without the energy input from an external source? I don't think so. Similarly, you will not see growth, learning, and success without challenges from the external environment. Nothing outside will change if your capacity to deal with them remains the same. Now this doesn't mean that you shouldn't be open to new opportunities and growth. Yes you must. The point here is that you must look for new opportunities and growth not out of frustration or conflicts or because you aren't able to figure out how to grow in your current role. You should look into new opportunities out of joy and knowing that you have transformed yourself as a person who has constantly demanded more from the self. Then, when there are problems in your new ventures, you will finish strong. Option number four—elevate the self—is the foundation of a successful work life.

In the world at large people advise us to disconnect with negative people, to surround yourself with people who uplift you and help you progress. This advice has ruined people's lives rather than empowering them. At your workplace, you have no idea if your boss is one of these toxic people you will inevitably encounter. What will you do if you haven't learned to deal with these types of people. You only know to keep away from them and disconnect with them. Are you planning to use the same strategy with your boss too? You know what it will get you into. And then, how many people are you going to disconnect with? Every person on this planet is good for your progress. The toxic and negative people teach you patience and help you to constantly improve yourself by looking inward. The positive people help you to look ahead and be focused. But if you disconnect with toxic people, you lose a major opportunity for success—self-improvement. My father would always advise me to be like the sun that spreads its rays to everyone. The sun never decided to disconnect with people who do not like it, criticize it, or don't value it. Imagine if the sun did that! The sun provides its light, warmth, and energy to all regardless of your behavior towards it. Similarly, life is a cluster of good and bad. You've got to know how to stay among everyone and move ahead. Your job as a leader is to spread sunshine to everyone. You must know how to stay positive around negativity.

Given the above advice, it is still imperative to safeguard your positive energy while being with the negatives of life. So how do you keep them at bay and yet not let their negative energies disturb you and your inner leader? Simply by elevating yourself inwardly in your thoughts and thinking like the ninety-two-year-old, petite, well-poised and proud lady, who is fully dressed each morning by eight o'clock, with her hair fashionably coiffed and makeup perfectly applied, even though she is legally blind. She moved to a nursing home today. Her husband of seventy years had recently passed away, making the move necessary. After many hours of waiting patiently in the lobby of the nursing home, she smiled sweetly when told her room was ready. As she maneuvered her walker to the elevator, the nurse provided a visual description of her tiny room, including the eyelet sheets that had been hung on her window. "I love it!" she said with the enthusiasm of an eight-year-old having just been presented with a new puppy.

"Mrs. Jones, you haven't seen the room ... just wait," said the nurse.
"That doesn't have anything to do with it," she replied.

"Happiness is something you decide on ahead of time. Whether I like my room or not doesn't depend on how the furniture is arranged, it's how I arrange my mind. I already decided to love it. It's a decision I make every morning when I wake up. I have a choice; I can spend the day in bed recounting the difficulty I have with the parts of my body that no longer work, or get out of bed and be thankful for the ones that do. Each day is a gift, and as long as my eyes open I'll focus on the new day and all the happy memories I've stored away, just for this time in my life."

It's all about how you arrange your mind. If you elevate yourself from within, outside circumstances and people's behavior cannot wither away your determination. You will be that leader that spreads sunshine to all. A ship does not sink because of the water around it; it sinks because of the water that enters into it. Similarly, you give up and fail not because of what's around you but because of what you allowed to enter within you. When you elevate the inner self, you can deal with anything, and you begin to receive more, to give more, to endure more, to embrace more, and to accept more. Poet Allama Iqbal said it best: "Elevate yourself so high that even God, before issuing every decree of destiny, should ask you: Tell me, what is your wish my child?" It's only when you elevate the self from within that you can achieve unstoppable success in any economy. Has anyone ever told you that you're too short, too tall, not smart enough, not CEO material, not the entrepreneur type, or just simply not good enough? There will always be people in your life that will give you a million reasons why you cannot achieve your goals. What is important is what you tell yourself. Do you say to yourself, "Well, nothing good ever happens to me," "I don't think I'll ever get that manager's position," or "I might as well file bankruptcy; I don't see a way to sustain this business." Your low expectations of yourself will trap you into remaining average. Elevating yourself is about believing in your potential and exceeding what people expect of you. It's about increasing your capacity to create success and deal with failure.

Julia's Story

I recall my coaching sessions with Julia, owner of a fitness center. Julia had been excellent at her work. She was aspirational and always looked for growth opportunities. But for the past year, her performance at work had been slowing down, and she was frustrated. She was even thinking of shutting down her business. This is when she hired me for personal business coaching.

During the session, I found out about an interesting element of her career. A year before, Julia had submitted a high-end proposal to be considered by various investors. She also shared her idea at the local Shark Tank (an award-winning entrepreneurial-themed reality show that has reinvigorated entrepreneurship in America). She wanted to grow big after playing it small for six years. She worked relentlessly towards the project, working day and night with her team, and got to deliver her proposal well before the deadline. Everyone praised her idea, but no investor came through. Julia felt like a loser. She started to talk to herself out of the business. She believed that it's a man's world out there and that being a woman was the reason things didn't go well for her. All of this began to impact the team and the business bottom line.

Many of us operate like Julia. We have the expertise, ideas, knowledge, and skills to deliver our best. Yet we fall short of results. This is because our capacity to accept problems and failures is very small. We change paths (give up) when even a small obstacle comes our way. We get irritated at the slightest negative behavior or difficulty with people. I often tell my audience and clients that there is never a death of the business. It is the death of the leader from within. When you give up, when you engage in negative self-talk, when you doubt yourself, and when you begin to believe that it's over, everything in your professional life *will be* over. At whatever level you operate and in whatever state your inner leader is, that's how your professional life will shape up.

I had an opportunity to get to know Elaine Cheong, Vice President at Bank of America and President of the Ascend Philadelphia Chapter. During our conversation about business complexities, uncertainty, changes, and how she navigated to get to where she wants to be, she said,

You may have heard the phrase, "the only thing that is constant is change." For me, change is my friend. It has offered me enormous opportunities to acquire new skills, engage in steep learning curves while I push myself to emotional, and psychological limits to chart new and exciting career paths. My attitude towards failure may have something to do with the healthy optimism that I carry with me. Being brought up in the Eastern culture, there is a profound acceptance of the balance of yin and yang and the law of cause and effect that permeates everything in the universe. My equilibrium is a place where I must exercise steady control and willpower with an unwavering commitment towards accomplishment of the goal. There is no question that no matter what talents you are born with, there is no compromise for hard work and dedication; these are the fundamental building blocks, and the seed one must sow to reap the fruits of success, lest your talents amount to nothing. I realized early on that failure is not an option for me, but that failure is not failure at all if I can learn from the experience, and most importantly, have the capacity to build grit and perseverance as the fuel needed to propel me forward. Trying to define success in the absence of failure is like trying to describe something in a vacuum. Faced with change, one's ability to adapt and learn, and live a life filled with direction and conviction is the key to sustained success however you define it.

How true, I thought to myself. It reminded me of how I, too, constantly challenge my team to believe in change and overcome failure. I want them to bring new, innovative, and disruptive ideas to the table in addition to their regularly scheduled responsibilities. I want them to feel comfortable trying things, even if they fail, so that we can all learn together. I want them to minimize their busy work and maximize their truly impactful contributions to our organization. And this is possible when they first elevate their inner leader. I firmly believe that this is critically important to the careers and professional development of all. The reason you are where you are today is because of how much you have elevated yourself in the past. What your future will look like will be decided on how much you elevate the self today. The level to which you elevate yourself is the level at which your income, business, people, clients, and company will operate. It will be seen in your organization's culture. If you do your part, the universe will do its part.

I still remember a cold wintery day in December 2012 when something inside of me changed as a leader. I was traveling to New York to deliver a keynote whose invitation came unexpectedly right before the holiday season. After successfully delivering the keynote, on my way back to the New York airport, I stopped at a small Italian roadside restaurant to pick up some food for the trip. The owner of the restaurant greeted me with a huge smile, welcomed me to New York and asked me my name as she handed me the menu. By now I was already impressed with the cleanliness on the inside. The owner offered me bottled water and some bread while I take a look at the menu. I went ahead and placed my to-go order. During the wait time, the owner spoke with great enthusiasm. And as we conversed, I was thinking to myself, "How is she so happy on this Christmas Eve serving me while everyone else is enjoying with their family?" As my to-go order was ready, I paid her the bill and added a good tip. But I couldn't step out without asking her the secret to her happiness. She looked at me, smiled, and said, "Some years back I was leading a hand-to-mouth existence, struggling to find customers and competing with other restaurants in the area. Then one day I read an article in a magazine, and what stuck with me was an inspirational line that said: 'You can complain because roses have thorns or you can rejoice that thorns have roses.' From that day onwards I made a conscious choice to rejoice in my struggles, spread my wings and fly up high like an eagle. I changed myself internally, and that brought about changes in my actions and in my external world. Today I no longer struggle for customers. My clients have my card, and they call me when they need their to-go order or to book a table. I realized the only thing you have complete control over is your attitude. You alone are responsible for making yourself successful and happy." As she waved me goodnight, I could clearly see how she had changed her results. She had consciously awakened the leader within and had led herself to success. She had elevated herself.

Each of us can spread our wings and fly high like an eagle. Yet in reality, only a few of us manage to fly high. For most of us getting through the day is a challenge. This is because we condemn ourselves more often than elevate, and negativity overtakes our thoughts. We become remote controlled in the hands of people and circumstances. Our culture and the corporate world teach us to lead our teams, family, business, and clients. However, these are secondary. First, you've got to lead yourself. Lead your thinking, emotions, actions, and energy. You've got to awaken the leader within you.

It's said that one day, Frederick the Great of Prussia was walking on the outskirts of Berlin when he encountered a very old man walking ramrod-straight in the opposite direction.

"Who are you?" Frederick asked his subject.

"I am a king," replied the old man.

"A king!" laughed Frederick. "Over what kingdom do you reign?"

"Over myself," was the proud old man's reply.

Each of us is "monarch" over our own lives. We are responsible for ruling our actions and decisions. If you do not elevate the self, you will struggle to guide and lead others. Pull yourself out of difficulties by yourself.

The Impact of the Aura

Have you observed how even when the leader isn't highly visible—for example, the CEO who works behind closed doors on an upper floor—their attitude and their energy still affect the moods of their direct reports, and a domino effect ripples throughout the company's emotional climate. How does this happen? There is an interesting reasoning behind this called the *aura*. Each of us has our own aura. The aura is a subtle field of luminous multicolored energy that surrounds you. It is the natural energy form that radiates from your body. It's an extension of your inner self. You cannot see an aura with just your eyes, but bioelectrophotography captures these energy fields as a permeating light around the body. Aura reading machines have been developed too, though their effectiveness is still debatable. But you can feel it. Think about this—how many times has it happened that a leader enters the room and you can feel a burst of positive energy floating around him, touching each and everyone standing or sitting near him. Even before someone says a single word, you know that person means business and knows how to get the job done. Even before your first interaction with your client or boss, you have become their admirer; you want to work with them. How is that possible? It is because of the aura a person carries with them. Everyone's aura is as unique as his or her own fingerprints.

What is interesting is that the aura you bring to work each day has an impact on your workplace. Auras are always changing. The problems in workplace relationships happen when energies that were once alike or in harmony now change or vibrate at different frequencies. How many times have you walked away from a conversation feeling exhausted? Think of what happens when you see that person's name on an incoming call: your stomach sinks. This may have been the same person with whom you once shared an excellent bond.

When you are overwhelmed and feeling anxious or downtrodden, your energy can completely overtake another person's energy. I have had many opportunities to speak with people from the medical fraternity. During one of my talks in Dallas with a group of doctors who were heart specialists, I asked, "What is the one thing that you experience almost every day in your profession, more than any other?" I got various answers, but one of them nailed it. One doctor said aloud the word, "pain."

"True," I responded. "People in the medical field are dealing every day, every minute with the pain of their patients and their families. Not just the physical pain, but the emotional pain that the patient and their family bring in. The emotional pain of anxiety, worry, financial tensions, the fear of treatment, and sadness. At this point their energy level, their aura, is low and muscles are tight. This is why most doctors tell you to relax before any medical procedures or while measuring your vitals. Now when you, as a doctor, come in contact with the patient who is already in a disturbed state of mind, how imperative it is for you as a healer to ensure that your state of mind is not disturbed. Because a disturbed leader is a disturbed healer."

This is true for each of us. If you create thoughts of disturbance, first, you become vulnerable to absorbing the negativity around you. Second, every person around you can feel it, and your aura begins to disturb everyone. Does this mean someone can steal your energy from you? No. This is where your capacity comes to the rescue. You've got to elevate your aura, your level, and capacity so that you don't take on someone else's negativity and low energy upon yourself.

Elevating Your Thoughts

So how does one elevate the self? In the business world, we have been trained to elevate the self by learning more, expanding our connections, increasing competence and commitment, and honing our expertise. However, you will observe in your life that whenever situations at work arise, increase in intellectual capacity does little if you haven't upgraded your thoughts. Your thoughts are the roots of success and failure. As a leader, your job is to lead people, teams, budget, and the organization to an optimal level. For you to be successful at your work, to move on from one project to another and one failure to another requires a continuous flow of enthusiasm. Achieving what you want and reaching your destination depends upon the thoughts and aura that you carry on this journey. You may ask here, how are these the cause of my results? Take a pause here to reflect on a problem that you are facing at your workplace and want it resolved. It can be a situation or a person's behavior. Maybe you have a brilliant idea but haven't been able to execute it well enough. I want you to now think of an action that you have taken to resolve that problem. Got one? Now when you see the results of your actions and you aren't satisfied with it, what do you do? You revisit your actions and work on reframing your strategies. Then, you see the results, and they do not match the amount of effort you have put in. So you go back and again to work on strategies and actions to change the results. And you continue in this way, which takes a lot of your time, effort, and money. Now take a step back. If you observe closely, you aren't getting the best results because you are missing the root cause of your actions: your thoughts (Figure 6.1).

Figure 6.1 *Event, Action, Results.*

Thoughts are subtle bundles of energy created in the factory of the mind. These are not visible to the naked eye, but fructify into actions. Hence, they are in dotted line.

When you think of sound leadership, you probably think of great actions—the various ways you serve your team and set your company up for success. But being a leader is about more than what we do; it's about what we think. Your thoughts about an event determine your actions, which in turn create a new event that we call outcome or results. An event has no meaning until you put a meaning on it.

Let me share a couple of incidents here that will deeply connect to how important it is for leaders to elevate themselves. Some years back, there was a news piece that talked about how things had looked grim aboard a Southwest Airlines flight, when about twenty minutes after it departed from New York, passengers heard what sounded like explosions. Debris from an engine failure had broken open a window. A female passenger was sucked into the hole where the window had been. While oxygen masks dangled, and passengers screaming and struggled to save the woman, the pilot's voice conveyed none of the panic aboard the flight. For her composure in this crisis, Tammie Jo Shults was invited to the White House, along with first officer Darren Ellisor, the three members of the flight crew, and a few of the passengers who donned virtual superhero capes after the plane lost that engine. Tammie wasn't honored just because of her degrees and training, she was praised for her "nerves of steel" during an emergency. Her thoughts during times of crisis kept her energy and focus level high, leading to her actions and the end result. She had elevated her inner leader.

Recently on my travel to India for a few speaking and coaching engagements, I met with an old friend of mine, Vihaan, who works as a training and development specialist in a well-known company. After seventeen years at this company, he had reached a point where he was ready to give up his job and get into the speaking and coaching industry. I asked him where he was on his plans to become an entrepreneur. Excitedly, he showed me all the books he was reading and the seminars he had attended for his personal development. I asked him again about where he had reached on his goals. He started to tell me of all the cut-throat competition in India in this industry, of all the pressure to be visible on social media, and how the negativity and pressure wasn't allowing him to take his actions.

During this trip, I also met with Mr. Gopal, a lawyer by profession, and the chairman of a well-known and highly prestigious management association. Every problem that would come his way seemed to just disappear. He would constantly face issues with team underperformance and work politics. Yet what remained constant was his smile and joyful nature. How did he manage to navigate through negativity and challenges and get his results in the same country and state where Vihaan remained gripped by them? As Mr. Gopal told me one day, "By preparing myself a bit before I step into a situation I know might be negative, I'm bringing awareness to how I might feel at the end of the conversation and gaining the perspective I need not to let the negativity impact me." This can happen only when you constantly elevate yourself from within, and the situation on the outside then does not affect you. Only then can you experience unstoppable success.

Are there people who constantly criticize you, tell you that you can't do things, make you feel bad about yourself, even yell at you? Many of us decide to cut off these so-called "toxic" people. But think about it. What if toxic people are your team or bosses? How do you shut them out? And how many people are you going to shut out? It's time to elevate your inner leader so you don't avoid or ignore toxic people and situations; rather, you effectively deal with them. You may have been hurt by your peers, boss, or faced miserable conditions at work. You may be feeling like a failure or may have given up hope of becoming the next CEO. Your business might be failing, or you might be unable to expand and build the empire you wish. We associate our present experience with our thoughts about the past and make up a future that's negative. Stop doing that. Instead, begin to raise your thought frequency.

Today's corporate leaders must be potent pioneers—blazing new paths, dealing with uncertainties and having the courage to see them all the way through to the end. We need leaders who think big and envision the impossible. Decision-making is ultimately what you'll be judged on as a leader, as your choices could determine the overall success of the organization. You cannot make the best decisions when you are operating from lower levels of thinking. If you want to change your life and experience the fullness of life, you must begin to change your thought programming. To change your programming, you must learn the three-step technique I call ACC—absorbing, culling, channelizing.

1. **Absorbing:** This step is designed to replace the old negative data with new and uplifting information. The way to do this is to take in or absorb new data, data that is conducive to your success. Where can you get this data? It can come from any source you choose. For instance, let's say each day you read something that has encouraging information that inspires you and helps you to achieve greatness in your life, then obviously this is the data you want to read. But let me warn you of something here. These changes will not be easy at first. You may still resort to your old thoughts. This is where step number two comes in—culling. When you first replace your old beliefs with new beliefs, you will have to monitor your thoughts and what you read on a daily basis so you don't accidentally reverse the procedure. Your old thoughts will come rushing in, and you mustn't try to control or stop them. Just sit back and begin culling the thoughts.

2. **Culling:** It means to select from a large quantity. Just as you select the best vegetables and fruits, the best clothes, the best house, and the best job, similarly you should select the best thoughts. I remember having a conversation on this subject years ago with my father, when I asked him, "Do you think you can control your thoughts?" My father always taught me to never try and control my thoughts. He would often say that thoughts come and go of their own free will. The more you try to control them, the more you end up fighting with them. Rather, he would say to just decide which thoughts you want to live with—the ones that weigh you down or the ones that lift your spirits. Your

mind, like a river flowing downward, has a tendency to flow to the worst thoughts. But if you observe closely, thoughts don't come gushing out all at once. They begin as a single thought—a passing fearful thought, a fleeting memory, an exciting idea for the future, or an impulsive worry. As you build on this single thought and add more to it, more negative thoughts follow rapidly. Soon, they appear very big and hard to give up. So consciously begin to choose which thoughts you want to build on when they first appear.

3. **Channelizing:** Once you choose the thoughts that work in your favor, begin to channelize them. To channelize means to direct your thoughts in ways that improve your results. This can be done in three simple steps:
   - Think the same empowering thought every day.
   - Fully believe in your empowering thought.
   - Match your actions to your empowering thought.

How you want to see yourself in the near future is deeply influenced by your layer of thoughts. When thoughts change, results change. Your thoughts are like an echo that subtly influences your results. Training the mind to get the best thoughts begins with being more aware of your thoughts. Then, you can put a stop to the *very first* thoughts that arise, and substitute them with higher ones. The process itself is called "elevate your results" (see Figure 6.2).

Do you remember Julia's case (the fitness center owner) from earlier in the chapter? If she had elevated her thoughts, her results might have changed. In dealing with any situation or person, the very first thoughts

Figure 6.2   *Elevate Your Results.*

that you get about it are called the *beginner thoughts*. At this level, most of the thoughts are negative as they are almost always purely emotional reactions. These thoughts disturb your peace and weaken your inner strength. When you act on these thoughts, the results are usually mediocre or even counterproductive. Examples of such thoughts include

This always happens with me.

    It's no good putting in the extra effort.

    My boss discriminates against me.

    There are no growth opportunities here.

    They are ignoring me because they are mad at me.

    I am not going to get this contract.

These were some of Julia's thoughts too. These thoughts actually cause you to play the blame game, stop striving for your goals, take any risks, take any massive positive actions, or believe in yourself. So I suggested to Julia to not act on the beginners thoughts that she had towards the situation or her boss. I encouraged her to elevate it to the next level called *intermediate thoughts*. At this level, you begin to think of more productive and necessary thoughts about the same person and situation. Mind you, I did not mention positive thoughts. It's about productive and necessary thoughts. You start by just reframing the beginner level thought. It took Julia almost thirty minutes to reframe the thought "There's no point working hard here," to "I know I didn't get the opportunity this time, but as long as I try my best, that's all that matters." This new thought made her take charge of her actions and emotions. She put it on herself to deliver the best no matter what. When you act on these intermediate thoughts, the results are still usually mediocre. I encouraged her to now give her best thought towards this same situation and person, which meant she had to elevate it to the highest level called *master thoughts*. It took her around an hour and thirty minutes to come up with the master-level thoughts about her situation and boss:

Maybe my boss forgot to appreciate my work this time.

I should discuss this issue with him face to face and resolve it.

I will keep doing my best until I reach my goal.

These are just obstacles thrown my way to teach me how to grow.

These situations are the fertile ground for my success.

This brought about a change in her energy level and actions leading to massive productive results and making her unstoppable. I encourage you to go ahead and try it. Close your eyes, think about a problem or person you're trying to deal with, create the beginner thought, and elevate it to the intermediate level. Now from the intermediate level, take it to the master level. Catch the master-level thought, weigh its pros and cons and then act on it. I assure you, you will get your highest and best results, thereby making you unstoppable.

What have you got to lose? Start elevating the self now. Elevate your thoughts, your passions, your desires, your actions, your results, your grit, your endurance, and your inner leader. You can elevate your results when you elevate yourself. Today the main cause of burnout and stress at the workplace is not the work pressure, but an overburdened and over-informed mind. Think about it, business problems and challenges always existed. What has changed is their number and degree. But what has not change is our capacity to deal with these problems. With so much negative information being circulated, and with the increase in uncertainty, the quality of our thoughts has started to degrade. Let's begin by asking ourselves an important question, "What drains my mind power?" Our mind power and energy is depleted each day not because of work, but purely because of our inability to manage our thoughts. The more adulterated your thoughts, the lower your creativity and innovation power. A great deal of planning and energy goes into mulling over impoverished thoughts like revenge, complaints, corporate games, jealousy, favoritism, gossip, and backstabbing. With a drained out thought battery, how far are you going to go?

These days, wherever I travel, airports, hotels, and cabs have made charging the phone so simple and accessible. Why? Because they know you really can't go too far with a discharged phone. Our mind batteries are getting depleted, and I seldom see leaders and entrepreneurs charging theirs. You won't go very far in your industry if you do not elevate yourself using the power of your mind. Seldom do we use the power of mind in our professional life. Your thoughts have the power to allow a problem to use 70% of your energy in the moment or bring it down to 10%. One of the biggest mistakes we can make is taking the mind for granted. It's time to realize its importance in our workplace. It's time to become unstoppable. Here is a powerful mantra to remind yourself each day that you have limitless capacity. When you repeat this mantra daily, it is bound to help you elevate your inner leader and make it powerful beyond the circumstances. My father always told me that you get not what you want but what you deserve. So raise yourself to such a height that you deserve the best. And when you do elevate yourself, remind yourself of these words of wisdom by the poet Kabira: "Don't be like a date tree, which is very tall but provides neither shade to the weary traveller nor fruits within reach." When you elevate yourself, help others to rise and be of utmost use. Ultimately, this is how you and your organization will grow.

Mantra: "My ability to succeed is limitless today."

MANTRA 7

Enjoy Your Season

In America, it was still the tail end of winter in March of 2019. I had just returned from delivering a workshop in Australia, where it had been cool and rainy with a temperature of 73°F. It had been lovely there. I have never been a big admirer of the winter season. Summer is my best. What's your favorite season? After returning home, I had put a hold on my travel for the upcoming three weeks as Ashish, my husband, was planning his travel to India to work on one of his critical office projects. I was eagerly looking forward to these three weeks to stay put in America and complete this book as well as all the speaking and coaching sessions my admin had booked on my calendar. My husband left for India later that week on a Sunday afternoon. Sunday is also a day where I work out my plans for the week ahead, and I had it all perfectly articulated. My daughters and I settled in for dinner at seven pm. Just as we were about to begin our eating, I got a call from my father with the shocking news that my mother had been hospitalized due to a massive heart attack. I felt numb as my father explained to me what had happened. As I stayed on the phone, the food being left aside, I began looking for options on how to reach India. The distance between the U.S. East Coast and India is a good 8,448 miles by air. Most immigrants live with the fear of possibly not reaching home in time for the passing of loved ones or to deal with other family crises. I admit I live with this fear. With my husband on the flight to India, I was feeling rattled by the thought that I wouldn't be able to leave the girls and reach my mother on time. Just then something miraculous happened. My husband, who was in flight, suddenly got the WIFI connection, and my younger daughter was able to get him on phone messaging and explain what had happened. As my husband's plane landed in Paris for a connection to India, he called me, and we exchanged notes. This being an emergency; he agreed to cancel his travel to India and come back to America so I could leave.

Soon I was in flight to Mumbai, India, and landed there to be with my family. Things were tough while there but we were determined to come out of these tough times. My mother began to recover and was able to go home. I decided to stay with her until she was fully healthy again. Thankfully, I am blessed with supportive clients who understood my situation and rescheduled their sessions with my team. Meanwhile, as I was enjoying my time with my parents and the hot summer of Mumbai, I got a couple of great speaking offers while there. Things went by smoothly and after a month I was back to my home in America as spring was setting in. It felt as though my life had been through a time lapse.

On my flight back to America, I realized that in a month's time I had experienced four different seasons: the rainy season of Australia, the winter in America, the summer in India and the onset of spring in America. I don't think many may have experienced a change in season so rapid. And while I may have my preference of season, I clearly did not have a choice of which season to stay in during this set of adventures. Each season I experienced in this compressed time frame had its own beauty, challenges, and purpose. The season of Australia was beautiful and favorable for my speaking. The winter of America was bitter but compressed with many sessions lined up. Summer in India was extremely humid and challenging while handling personal commitments and getting through tough times. The onset of spring in America breathed a renewed energy into me. This phase of my life taught me very valuable lessons. I realized that each of us have our favorite seasons, but we must pass through each season; that the seasons of life are very unpredictable and impermanent; that each season brings with it its own hopes, desires challenges, and opportunities. And this experience also broke my long-standing myth about winters being the most challenging. Summer, my favorite season, brought with it its own challenges. To top it all off, I learned that each season of life brings with it an ending, a period of confusion and distress as we begin a new season. What matters most is—do you just go through each season or do you grow in each season?

The Season of Silence

In our work life, we face numerous seasons: slow economy seasons, conflict-filled seasons, opportunity- and problem-rich seasons, retirement seasons, growth and learning seasons, and promotion and layoff seasons. The toughest season of all is the season of silence. This is a time when you are working hard, putting in the effort, and yet you see no results. You may think that if only you saw some improvements, at least you'd know that what you are doing is helping. But you've got to know that most of the time before things come to pass, there is a season of silence where you are not seeing anything changing. It seems the needle just doesn't move. Did you know that it is during the season of silence that most people across the globe get discouraged and give up on their dreams? What we don't realize is this: while you are putting in the effort, behind the scenes changes are taking place. The universe is lining up the right opportunities—like that promotion or the right people you need. So while you are passing through the season of silence, dig in your heels and believe that you will see the results. As the biblical scriptures read, "And let us not be weary in well doing: for in due season we shall reap, if we faint not." Don't give up just because you don't see anything happening on the outside. Know that a lot is happening inside. Just as a seed takes root inside the ground in darkness, your results are shaping up in the season of silence. Trust your actions, trust the process, and most of all trust the success within you.

We all experience change and transition in life. Sometimes, the season of life is exciting and dynamic, and we feel on top of the world. At other times, we just want to go away and escape the situation. No season lasts forever. Genesis 8:22 says, "As long as the earth remains, there will be springtime and harvest, winter and summer, day and night." The problem is we prefer certain seasons over others and want to stay and operate in our favorite season. How often have you said, "I just can't wait for this season to be over." This phrase is clearly a sign that you aren't enjoying the season you're in. Your work life has seasons that constantly change and that is what makes it fascinating. Imagine if your work were to remain the same forever, would you treasure positive and happy moments of your work life? Nothing is permanent in this world and so never take any season too seriously. I would often complain to my father of how I hated the winter season. To which he would ask me "How is this hate helping you?" He would remind me of the purpose of the season: "The season isn't concerned whether you like it or not. But remember, the season you curse is a blessing to someone somewhere. You will never get this season back again in the same year. So, learn to enjoy while you are in it. And remember that a season is never good or bad. It's all about what you make of it." These words, as I reflect on them even today, became the cornerstone of my success. It taught me how to live and thrive in each season.

Maximize the Season You're In

When I say enjoy the season, you're in, I realize that every season isn't a summer vacation party. Not every season is one where the economy is booming and people are at their best. I get that. But seasonal changes can still be enjoyed to the fullest. Every day that you live with a negative, defeated attitude is a day that you have wasted. You cannot change the season's timetable, but you can change your own attitude. Never run away from a season. Face it and come out stronger, happier, healthier, and better prepared for the next season in your life. There is a winner in you. You were created to be a master of your craft. Too often we allow a difficult season in our lives to limit us and convince us to settle where we are. In my career, I have gone through a lot of these difficult seasons. But I learned to grow through them simply by making friends with Mr. Success thoughts and keeping Mr. Failure thoughts away. Success thoughts travel slowly in your mind, and don't build up too much on one another. They keep you calm, relaxed, and internally motivated. Failure thoughts are the ones that travel too fast and build up on each other. They often paralyze your decision-making and keep you from moving ahead in your season.

I do not know what season of your life you are in. But I do know with full conviction that this is YOUR season. It's meant for you. It's been given specially to you. Because if you ever wished for success, the seasons of failure and disappointment are here for you. If you wished to learn patience, your season is blooming with people who will push you to the limits and annoy you to the ends of the earth. And don't worry about how long the season lasts. It may stay with you for three months, six months, or three years. Put your shoulders back, hold your head high up, and walk with confidence in every season. You can thrive in every season with the 3C technique: change, compute, and canonize.

1. **Change your focus:** Each season brings new opportunities and challenges. Avoid focusing on the things you don't like about a season and focus on all the things that are wonderful about the season.

2. **Compute your blessings:** Make a decision today to be thankful for at least one blessing every day of the year. Complaining won't change your season. When you begin to compute your blessings daily, you begin to make the most out of every season that comes into your life. Start with daily blessings—waking up healthy, your breath, opportunity to interact with people, a cup of coffee, your team, a compliment received, your physical and mental abilities, your job, and your income. There are millions of people who might be wanting the job you already have.

3. **Canonize your language:** There is great strength in positive language. Incredible things happen when you change your language. Instead of saying, "I've so much work to do this week," say "I know I have lots to complete, but I'm going to do my best and get through like a winner." Check your language. Do you catch yourself often saying, "I hate driving daily in this traffic to meet with clients," or "I don't like the people I work around," or "My job and boss suck." If this sounds familiar, it's time to canonize your language.

Never let the season you are in define who you are. Don't change what you believe according to what season you are in. People often make wrong decisions in tough seasons and emotional decisions during thriving seasons. When you are in a challenging or difficult season, be careful what meaning you give things. I remember during the early years of my career, in my role as a human resource manager in a giant corporation, I recruited two management trainees: Aaron, an Irish immigrant, and Nianzu, an immigrant from China. Both were happy with their jobs, and the company was satisfied with their overall work performance. Things were moving well until the company decided to restructure and downsize by closing a few projects. Unfortunately, we had to let go of Aaron and Nianzu along with 250 other employees. Now I do not know what happened to the rest of the people that were let go, but I did happen to meet Aaron three years later at a local grocery store. I asked him how he was doing. He told me how things were tough for him after he lost his job and no one was willing to give a chance to someone with only three months of work experience. With no family and friend support in this country, he went for days with no food and money. At times, he was living on food stamps. He soon took up a packaging and filling machine operator's day job and drove a taxi in the evening to support his basic needs. All of this despite his management degree. Late at night, he would hunt for jobs of his caliber. Things began to change after a year and a half when Aaron was driving his cab and a passenger was the owner of a start-up company. During his conversation, the passenger got to know about Aaron's skills in managing business and people. He was impressed with the solutions Aaron shared with him on a few of the pressing challenges the company was going through. This man invited Aaron to his office the next week. That was it. Aaron got an offer, not to join as an employee but as a consultant to this start-up company. Today, Aaron is happy and well on his way to success. His season changed. And as for Nianzu, well, I heard from Aaron that Nianzu had gone into depression after months of unemployment and had headed back to China. As we exchanged email addresses and wished each other luck, I walked away confidently knowing that tough seasons do not last, but tough people do. It is during tough seasons that we learn new lessons both about the world and ourselves. We discover ourselves deeply. We develop the character to handle the success waiting to reward our perseverance. Just like the seasons change and the clouds give way to the sun, we must remember that so do our circumstances. No challenge, regardless of how intense, is permanent. Tough seasons don't last, but tough people do.

Navigating Seasonal Changes

Our job is to maximize the season we're in. Sometimes, we are too busy, too anxious, too fearful, and too worried to enjoy each season in life. We worry about our kids, our job, our age, our business, and our bank account. We worry if we will eat, if we lose our job even though we have a job, if we can pay our bills, and even if we now have the money. In all that worry, fear, anxiety, and rushing, we forget about the beauty of the season. Often, we appreciate it more when it is gone. I believe that through the seasons, nature sends us a powerful message that your life is a series of natural changes. Nothing ever stays the same. Your title, business, job, team, clients, and economy will all change someday. The important question is: are you prepared for the change in the season? Because the change in the season will always be beyond your control. Health may give way to sickness, promotion may give way to unemployment, pleasure may give way to pain, abundance may give way to poverty, honor may give way to disgrace, weakness may give way to strength, and failure may give way to success. When change comes, we must realize that it doesn't happen overnight. Transformation comes through a period of time, and there will be victories and setbacks. Be patient and allow everything in your life to run its course. I know how the season of setbacks always seems neverending and the season of victory forever seems short-lived. But it's not. Each season has its own cycle to complete. Nature never works in haste. But we humans are always in a rush to achieve, acquire, and be victorious. It is like a mad race. This puts us under pressure causing ill-health, fatigue, and frustration. As the famous Indian poet Kabira says, "Go slow O mind, everything happens at its own pace. The gardener may water with a hundred pots, but the fruit will arrive only in its season." Poet Kabira has acknowledged the importance of patience in life. You can't reap the harvest before time no matter how much effort you make. You have to have patience for the right season to come. The gardener pouring "a hundred pots of water" (extensive irrigation) will not hasten the arrival of the fruits; instead, they will ruin the process. Whatever you are working towards, be patient for the results and give your best in the current season and let your season come. Let your results manifest in the right season at the appropriate time. Always remind yourself that you are the only person who can make your life better in every season.

Every season brings with it one common element; the time to reflect and renew. When your season is soaring high, reflect and renew. When you are going through a difficult season, reflect and renew. Most leaders and entrepreneurs reflect and renew only during tough times. We forget that good times will soon pass away, the season will change and challenges will set in. So plan ahead by reflecting and renewing in all of your life's seasons.

The Universe Has a Bigger and Better Plan for You

Leaders are planners by nature. It's just a part of who we are. In what direction should I take my company? How are things going to turn out?

Where should I make investments? How can I expand my business? And there is no problem with planning, whether short term or long term. The problem sets in when your plan for the future interferes with your actions and state of mind today. It then robs you of the joy of today's season. We make our little plans, and if they do not work, we feel frustrated. And when things manifest to their best result, beyond our planning expectations, we rejoice and wonder at the miracles.

One of my clients was to be appointed as the CEO of a large organization. He must have been in his early forties at that time. He had made great plans ahead of time for this. He also moved into a bigger house. At the company's annual event, during the promotion announcement, to his shock someone else's name was announced as the CEO. His heart sank. And then something unbelievable happened. His name was added to the company's board of directors. He hadn't even imagined reaching to this level. The universe went beyond his plan.

In yet another instance, a young woman I'm acquainted with loved her job and had plans to grow in her career. She was talented and smart when it came to her work. However, she constantly had adjustment issues with people. Most of the time, she also outgrew her job and would land at a new company almost every three to four years. In her most recent job, she was laid off due to company downsizing. For some reason, as hard as she tried, she did not get any other job. She was aware that her season was very challenging. She decided to use that season to establish a sales agency to sell mobile homes. Her season now became even tougher with lack of capital, too much competition, and lack of business experience. She enrolled in courses to equip herself with the necessary knowledge. Smart and talented as she was, she figured out how to navigate this new business territory and started crossing over one obstacle after another to accomplish her goals. It's been eleven years since she started her agency, and she hasn't looked back ever since. When I asked her, what her greatest lesson in life was, she said, "You can make every experience in life into an enriching process, or you can use it to become more resistant towards life. You can complain about a season or rejoice. You must choose."

My father often tells me that if things happen as per your wish, that's great. And when they don't, that's even better because the universe is protecting you and planning something bigger and better for you. The universe has a master plan. Be ever willing to embrace this master plan. No matter how long you're booked into the future and how foolproof your plan seems, your plan still has limitations—human limitations. Take a minute and look around you. What do you see? If you are in a room, you will probably see a wall or a ceiling. And if you're outdoors, you will see the trees, buildings, or the sky. Your vision is limited to that wall, tree, and sky. So whatever plan you make is based on what you can see. Similarly, you have no idea about what's going to come your way the next month, week, or minute. You don't know what challenges and opportunities await you beyond your limited vision and thinking. Your preparation is therefore necessarily limited.

I experienced this years back on a family vacation to Paris. We booked our tickets in economy class, and we were off to the airport. At the airport, we found out that we had collected frequent flyer miles and that our tickets had been upgraded to business class. Wow! Did we plan for this. No. In those years, our budget did not allow us to think about traveling in business class. So here we were, heading for a vacation to London in business class. The universe knows how to surprise (and shock) you.

Now, I'm not advocating that planning isn't necessary. Planning is excellent. Arvind had it all planned out too. He knew exactly how his career life would be—a dream IT job in America, a huge house, a beautiful family, a luxury car, and a great life living the American Dream. He took his steps in the direction of his plan. He applied for a relocation from India to America through his existing consulting firm in India. He got the visa, and the next thing he knew he was in New York. He enjoyed his work in the tall office building in Manhattan. After two years of work, his family wanted him to settle down. Following the traditional arranged marriage concept of India, Arvind was married and went back to New York with his new family. Soon he had two children of his own and life was moving just as planned. He was happy with his life and planning skills. After five years with the company, Arvind made a new plan. He decided to switch to another company that would process his green card application so that finally he would be a U.S. citizen. Once the entire process was complete, he wanted to start his own business in Silicon Valley. He began the process by resigning from his current job to get into a company that promised to start his green card application. Arvind was doing just fine. The green card application process started. When U.S. Customs and Immigration asked Arvind to send over extra evidence for a green card application, the company lawyer sent them the files express. FedEx confirmed they'd arrived, but the government said it didn't have them. The process now got delayed, and Arvind's current work visa with the new company was set to expire in nine months. He got tense—very tense. The paperwork was re-sent, but by this time, the immigration policies had become more stringent. Finally, due to lack of evidence as demanded by U.S. Customs and Immigration, Arvind's green card had to be reapplied. He started the application process again. Meanwhile, his current working visa was extended yearly but with a sword potential rejection hanging over him. Finally, his green card was rejected, and he had to leave the country with his family and go back to his job in India. He did all that he could to make his plan work, but it clearly failed. This frustrated him, and he was stressed out. He then left his family in India and again came back to the United States, hoping for something positive to happen this time with the application. He wasn't willing to accept his season and the universe's big plan.

We plan something, we prepare our resources for it, and we make extra efforts so that no detail remains unconsidered, but our plans get canceled anyway. Isn't it frustrating when this happens? We end up sour-graping. We feel bad that others push through with their plans, but we weren't able to. Worse, we point the blame towards universe. After all, didn't we always hear that the universe promises to give us what we asked for in faith? So what I am saying is this: the plans you have made for yourself are good, keep making them. But know the universe's plans are ultimately far better.

What matters here is when the universe gives you a totally different plan or your plan gets delayed, what do you do? Do you get frustrated like Arvind? Or do you change your script and work alongside the universe like Steve Jobs? Steve Jobs is often quoted as saying that if he had never dropped out of college, he would have never dropped in on this calligraphy class, and personal computers might not have the wonderful typography that they do today. In one of his speeches, Jobs said, "You can't connect the dots looking forward; you can only connect them looking backwards. So you have to trust that the dots will somehow connect in your future. You have to trust in something—your gut, destiny, life, karma, whatever. This approach has never let me down, and it has made all the difference in my life."

This is what Arvind should have done. He should have taken a step back and connected the dots to see what the universe's plan was. But he continued to stay in the same role for twelve long years at the same salary only because he held on too tightly to his plan and did not accept the master plan of the universe, which could have saved him from many losses and taken him to a place bigger than where he was. He could have today been in a much better position in another company in India or elsewhere.

You see, for years I too lived a life where I focused only on the negative events and happenings of my day. I can't tell you how many of my golden years were ruined by me because of something that didn't go the way I had planned for it to go. For years, I let seasons pass by as I allowed my past to dictate my present and future. There were seasons in my life when no one supported me in my journey to success. There were seasons of loneliness, regret, and guilt. There were seasons when responsibilities at home were often in conflict with my success at work. With every incident in my life, job, and business, I did understand that our difficulties are tests and one must pass the test with good results. And I did. But sadly many of us fail miserably. The universe does the sorting out with these tests. It discovers who will stand firm and make progress even when storms loom over. It discovers who is willing to dance in the rain and do great things. It checks for those who are willing to change with change in season. Because that will determine their future. Do you look at things that are and think to yourself, "I will never get that promotion at work," or "I will never have more money in my business." What do you want in the future? What do you want your next season to be like? Thinking negatively not only puts your day at stake but your entire future as well. It's easy to talk positively and have faith when the season in our life is calm. It's quite different when trials and tribulations come in. I believe we lose a lot of battles strictly because of our negative thinking. I wonder how many times we all get storms in our lives and turn them into tornadoes by simply thinking negatively.

That is nothing that takes more self-control than not thinking negatively during challenges and tough times. To cross from one season to another with patience is a fruit of the spirit that we desperately need. There is a good hidden in every season. The storms of the seasons will be much easier to cross when you say to yourself that it's all for the best. This too shall pass. And along with this mantra, your need to do four things constantly:

1. **Keep moving ahead in tough seasons:** One day a young lady was driving along with her father. They came upon a storm, and the young lady asked her father, "What should I do?" He said, "Keep driving." Cars began to pull over to the side, the storm was getting worse. "What should I do?" the young lady asked. "Keep driving," her father replied. On up a few feet, she noticed that eighteen wheelers were also pulling over. She told her dad, "I must pull over, I can barely see ahead! It is terrible, and everyone is pulling over!" Her father told her, "Don't give up, just keep driving!" So, she kept on driving, and soon she could see a little more clearly. After a couple of miles she was again on dry road, and the sun came out. Her father said, "Now you can pull over and get out." She said, "But why now?" He said, "When you get out, look back at all the people who gave up and are still in the storm; because you never gave up your storm is now over."

How true. It takes courage, determination, and passion to keep moving forward when your strength seems to be failing you. Most of us will experience hard choices, stressful events, and difficult situations that will urge us to stop and give up what we are doing. Take a moment to consider where in your life you might have paused for a break in the season, and never gotten back to it. Whatever be the season, keep moving ahead. Don't simply wait for the season to change. Take your actions and soon you will see a change in your season. Never give up in the midst of any season.

2. **Take it easy in all seasons:** A widow had two sons on whom she relied for financial support. One son sold umbrellas. The first thing the mother did every morning was to look out to see if the sun was shining or if it looked like it was going to rain. If it was cloudy, her spirits were good because there was a chance that it might rain and her son would sell some umbrellas. But if the sun was shining, she was miserable all day because no umbrellas would be sold. The widow's other son sold fans. Every morning that it looked like rain, she would get depressed because without the sun's heat, no one was likely to buy fans. No matter what the weather was, the widow had something to fret about. While commiserating with a friend one day, the friend remarked, "Perk up. You've got it made. If the sun is shining, people will buy fans; if it rains, they'll buy umbrellas. All you have to do is change your attitude. You can't lose." When that simple thought sank in, the widow lived happily ever after. Like this widow, we too are either full of anxiety or excitement about the season that has to come that we don't laugh often, we don't give our best, and we don't relax. In short, we don't enjoy the season we are in. We live with a "what if" syndrome. We await the next season and complain about it when it's here because it did not turn out as anticipated. We dread the changing seasons of our life as we expect only bad or unpleasant things to happen. We operate like chicken little as if the sky is falling and it's falling on us. I agree that no every

day is sunshine and rainbows, but that dark clouds will also be in your path. We cannot avoid them. But seasons are meant to be enjoyed. Always take it easy and wear a smile in every season that you pass through. One day we will find ourselves on our deathbed and, looking back, realize that we were so focused on how the future would look that we never experienced or savored the present. I often remind myself of a quote by Mother Teresa that says: "Yesterday is over, tomorrow is not promised. We only have today." Every season gives you deeper roots. It prepares you for the next.

3. **Keep faith in every season:** As you move from one season to another, so will your emotions. But your faith must be constant. Faith in yourself and in the power above. Some years ago, I was working as a regional director, coaching and training in my role. I wasn't even planning about being a global speaker and author. But things went downhill for me when the new CIO joined the company. With the new policies and structure in place, I outgrew my job and felt stuck. I decided to use this season of mine to take a leap of faith and expect good things to happen. I resigned from my role and took the path of entrepreneurship. Amazing things happened on the way, and I began passing through many seasons to get to where I am. How many of us in our job and business are willing to have faith that whatever be the season—it's for the best. That good things are happening and will happen again.

4. **Change with the season:** When we climb upwards into the uncrowded world of success, we discover that people up there have experienced many seasons. One of my closest friends is an extremely successful businessman. When you see him, you might think he got really lucky with so much wealth and success. In reality, behind this prosperous company is a man who fought his way upward. During the nine unbelievably challenging seasons it took him to succeed, I never heard him complain. The thing I heard him say most often was, "I'm changing with every season." And he did change for the better. Read the biographies

and autobiographies of legendary leaders. You will discover that each of these people changed their thinking and behavior with every change in season. They learn from every season. I have seen sales executives use stormy seasons to discover why they lost important sales. I have also seen businesses fail when the entrepreneur would not change with the change in the season. Many ambitious people fail to succeed because they don't try a new approach. In a new season, rather than changing their thoughts, behaviors, and strategies, they beat their heads against the wall and give up. Change with the change in season. Sometimes, it's a season of taking small steps towards your goal, and sometimes, it's a season to take a leap of faith to the next level.

Let's face it. The pressure of our modern work life constantly threatens to take a toll on our ethics and energy. But exceptional leaders are the ones who condition themselves for success in any season. It is said, "The future is yours for the taking." Yet only a few people grab their life with speed and enthusiasm. These few successful people have learned to give their best in every season. You do not hear them say, "When my season comes I will be better." Or, "I'll do my very best when the season changes for the better." Unfortunately, none of us know when the season will change and what our situation will be at that time. According to Ecclesiastes 3:1, "To everything there is a season; and a time for every purpose under the sun." Like the seasons themselves, one must be labile—always willing to readily undergo change. You truly cannot do much about your past or future season. The only season you can live in and give your best to is the season you are in. Never let it simply pass by. Start where you are, in whatever season you are. You already have everything you need to triumph in every season. The below mantra will help you to enjoy all the seasons in your work life.

Mantra: "This too shall pass. I will enjoy this season."

The Final Call

There have been a lot of challenges along the way. There were times when doubt cast a gloomy shadow over my aspirations and goals. Money became tight, and I wondered whether I would ever get off the ground. Sometimes, I thought it would be a lot easier to give up on my dreams and go back to my job. It certainly would have been easier, but I wouldn't have been truly fulfilled. For many years, that's what the pattern of my life had been, changing my track too soon. I now realized that if you give up on the things that matter most to you, you will likely establish a pattern of giving up on anything when things don't go the way you hoped. And worse, you end up feeling unfulfilled.

You, me, and everyone who is working for a purpose—whether a world-changing one or a purpose for the self—who desires to fulfill their goals and dreams, and who want to thrive at their work and are committed to taking the leap from average to exceptional, this is your final call. You have wasted enough of your time, energy, and potential in being average. You have heard enough of the opinions of people and acted according to their will. You've waited long enough for circumstances and people to change. Now is your time. Your time to succeed and thrive. Your time to do the things you've always wanted to do. It's time for you to motivate yourself to be an achiever. The Greek philosopher Plato said, "If people would move the world, they must first move themselves." The flight to your success is taking off, and this is your final call to board it. If you do not move, if you do not board this flight to success now, when will you? If you don't listen closely to this final call and board the flight to success, chances are you never will. And one day, you will look back at yourself knowing that the flight was waiting for you at your doorstep, the ticket (your dream) was with you, but you did not take the step. And that day you will be the only one who will feel disappointed at what you could have been by simply boarding the flight to success. Most people have been disappointed by what they did *not* do than what they *did* do. Move now. Start that business idea you have now, start studying for that degree/diploma now, start that charity or outreach program now, start writing that special song in your mind and singing it now, and start making that dream a reality now.

You may have been through challenging times in your professional life. We've all been tested. No matter what happened in your past, and how many mistakes you've made, you can still board the flight to success. And while on this flight to a land of endless possibilities, there will be turbulence. To get through the turbulence, remind yourself that your career life is too short. That you'd rather try and fail than live a life of regret. It's easy to give up on people, give up on the job, give up on your business, give up on a difficult company target, give up on your boss, give up on the economy, and give up on yourself.

But have you ever tried being a prisoner of hope? Now that's difficult but a true quality of an exceptional leader. Have you spent days together so full of hope and expectancy that you can't help believing for the best? You may have had a lot of things come against you. I know sometimes it seems like the more you work towards something, the further it gets away from you. Whatever the circumstances, I am telling you what I tell all executives and entrepreneurs: "Finish strong." Most of us start our journey towards success with great enthusiasm and a belief in winning. But the win does not happen for most of us. This is because we are not able to sustain the turbulence on the journey to success, and we give up. Realize that the reason the pressure seems to have turned up is because you are close, very close to success. I know how it feels when you are doing all the right things at work, going that extra mile, and yet you are passed over that promotion. I connect with your feeling of working tirelessly on your business yet not getting any clients. But it's important to remind yourself that you *can* finish strong what you started.

John Stephen Akhwari, a marathon runner who represented Tanzania in the marathon in 1968, stands a testimony to the importance of finishing strong. During the race, he succumbed to cramps that slowed his progress. Most observers, seeing his injuries, assumed he would pull out and go to the hospital. Instead, he received medical attention and returned to the track to continue the race. His pace, of course, was now much slower, but his resolve to complete the event remained intact. Akhwari crossed the line in last place. He was asked why he'd carried on, even when he knew he would never win, and his response has gone down in sporting history. "My country did not send me 5,000 miles to start the race," he said. "They sent me 5,000 miles to finish the race." What is your race? Have you started on a new project, new business, new relationship, new job, new team, and new department? Then, make a resolve today that you are going to finish strong regardless of the adversity you face. This is your final call. Will you make history or become history?

I believe we are born to succeed. Having traveled around the world, I have seen that people give up the hope and expectancy of being successful. And because they come to work with this attitude daily, organizations aren't seeing exponential growth. Every mantra in this book that I have written builds up on the previous one and is bound to help you finish strong. When in difficulty, when you want an answer to your problem, open any page and you will find a solution. Put your finger on any mantra, and it will reveal to you your next step.

Every moment you have at your work is divine, a gift you have been blessed with, and how easily it could be taken away from you. Today may be the last day of your life, for no one knows what might happen tomorrow. Now every day I look back and ask myself, "If I died today, would I be satisfied with the life I have lived?" This makes me give my best each day. Today onwards, know that this is your final call. Board your flight to unstoppable success before it takes off. Get to where you are supposed to be. I want you to have a bigger vision for yourself. I want you to step into your greatness now and do the things you want to do, be the person you want to be. Your future is very bright. It's your time to succeed. It's your time to take the leap from average to exceptional. Don't go around with low self-esteem, thinking that you don't have what it takes. You are fully loaded with *I-Power*. Start with the *I*. Condition it for success each day with these seven mantras. Use this power in every area of your life. Awaken it and you will begin to see the transformation in yourself and in your outcomes. Use *I-Power* to think big, dream big, and achieve big. When one dream dies, have the courage to dream another dream. Try something else. We were all born with this amazing *I-Power*. Most people go through their work life without acknowledging their *I-Power*. They choose to conform with the crowd and just be average, living a nine-to-five life. But a handful of people start with the *I,* choose to live life to a higher standard and become successful. Peter the Great of Russia said, "He who conquers others is strong; he who conquers himself is mighty." A leader's role is so important, you owe it to yourself and your people to continually evolve as an exceptional leader.

Time waits for no one. If you are alive today, if you've gotten out of bed today, then make today count. It's your day today to change your own life and get yourself a step closer to your dreams and goals. It's a final call to do anything your heart desires. We take things for granted and then they are gone, gone forever. They become a fading wisp of the past. We ignore so much of the goodness that our work life offers us, only missing it when it is gone. You think you can always write a book or climb those mountains or become a CEO, and then, you realize that the door has closed, and the window is sealed. Trust me, today is the day that will never come back tomorrow. The world will never have a chance to be exposed to your greatness and talents if you do not motivate yourself now to deliver what you are here for.

You may have plenty of reasons to give up on your dreams, but remember, the universe did not bring you this far to leave you. Stop settling for mediocrity. Stop being average. You have success within you. You are born for greatness. Don't let anyone talk you out of it. The success within is greater than all the storms and setbacks around you. You are designed to be unstoppable. You are here to achieve success. Make every single day at your work count. Leave a legacy every day at your work. Be excellent at your workplace. Do everything with your whole heart and soul. Lead yourself and your organization to success. Turn every obstacle into an opportunity. It's your time to rise higher, accomplish your goals, and be everything you were created to be. Keep moving forward. Never ever quit until you are living the life you once dreamed of. This is your time. Transform your destiny. Let nothing break you. Let nothing stop you. Become unstoppable no matter the economy. No matter who supports you and no matter what happens in your life. And as you navigate through your job and business, know that it's possible to achieve unstoppable success. Know that it's not over until you achieve what you want to achieve.

Don't exit from your workplace and from the world without leaving your trace. I urge you today to think about what will be different because you came this way. Take this as a final call to craft experiences now. The final call to express your love to your people, to resolve workplace conflicts, to write a book, to dance in the rain, to climb a mountain, and to cross a river. And as you awaken the *I-Power* within you, as you heed the final call and board your flight to success, to being exceptional, remember you are unstoppable—today and forever.

Index